An Incredible Life

Best in the History of the World

— by Ray Johnson —

DORRANCE PUBLISHING CO
EST. 1920
PITTSBURGH, PENNSYLVANIA 15238

Dorrance Publishing Co
585 Alpha Drive
Suite 103
Pittsburgh, PA 15238
Visit our website at *www.dorrancebookstore.com*

ISBN: 979-8-88925-179-8
eISBN: 979-8-88925-679-3

Astounding, amazing, impossible, truly, how millions of individuals across our nation and the world suddenly found themselves fascinated by the life and story of a regular working-class teenager from a non-famous family from the state of Utah.

Intriguing how famous an inventor, author, object of dozens of national magazine cover photo stories and feature articles, internet sensation, idol and hero to many materialized so unexpectedly.

Fans ringing the telephone non-stop day and night, flooding the mail, traveling long distances just to meet, from every state all across the country and from numerous other nations.

Why? How did a complete unknown obscurity explode into such widespread heralded recognition and fame?

National magazines taking the kid all over parts of the world, staying often in expensive hotels and eating in the finest restaurants.

Advertised on TV, radio, and in newspapers as the special guest speaker at national conventions and shows, used in TV commercials and ads. This is my life story.

Our family made Flaming Gorge famous the very first season it opened to fishing after the dam was completed and the reservoir began to fill with water from the Green River above.

My dad read in the newspaper that the new fishery should be great fishing for 2-3 lb. rainbow trout which had been planted the past couple years as the lake began to fill.

So, he took our family up there and at first caught the rainbows from shore down in the Utah portion of the lake.

But I had read one paragraph in the paper stating that Wyoming had been planting some brown trout up where the Green River entered the lake. So, I talked him into taking our relative's small 12-foot aluminum boat with us. After we caught the rainbows in Utah, he and I started trolling in the boat with my lures nearly 100 miles farther north at Buckboard Crossing boat ramp. There wasn't any marina there yet then.

We trolled miles along The Big Bend shoreline without a single bite, after catching rainbows fast early from shore down in Utah. So, he wanted to quit and leave, but I saw a big rock slide up ahead and asked him to try it first. Bam! We caught a nine lb. brown there.

We could see the only island on that end of the lake a short distance away from the rock slide and decided to try it. Bonanza! We caught our limits of 4-12 lb. browns quickly trolling my lures around the deep end of the island.

In those days, the limit was eight per person with no weight restriction. When we got back to Salt Lake, the TV, radio and newspaper reports were all about our totally unexpected huge haul catch of the big trophy browns, when only small rainbows had been publicized as the anticipated catch on the new bi-state reservoir.

Though only a young teenager, I started traveling to and fishing The Gorge for the big browns every chance I got or could invent.

National magazines started printing feature articles about me catching those trophy browns. For the first few years I only caught any of them in the far upper portions of the lake between the river entry confluence and Squaw Hollow.

Then Lucerne Marina down on the middle portion of the lake phoned me and asked me to please come down there to their area with my national magazine and TV reporters to get them some publicity, because so far it was all about catching the trophy fish much farther up the lake in The Buckboard areas.

So, I invited writers and TV reporters down to see if we could catch any of them at Jerry Taylor's Lucerne Marina area where none had ever been reported caught yet.

I was a gutsy brash teenager at that time. Though I had never fished on any part of the lake in that area, I told them all we would go catch the new Utah Lake Record Brown that very day. Of course, they all scoffed at that.

We started trolling my lure just with one line right out of the marina bay around the Lucerne Campground point: "lightening instantly struck" ... unbelievably I caught a 12 lb. brown trout immediately, which at that time was the largest yet reported ever caught on the Utah portions of the lake.

A young couple fishing on the shore filmed it jumping all over the surface (many people don't think brown trout jump, but many large ones repeatedly do).

They had a motor bike, so I asked them to let me hop on with the fish and give me a ride back to the marina store.

Jerry Taylor and the news media were dumbfounded, speechless. This was like just minutes after I left them and started to fish... impossible, but I actually did it even better and quicker than I had bragged that I would.

A few big browns started being caught in that middle section of the lake, but not many.

We still caught nearly all on the upper Wyoming portion of the lake. I caught dozens, then hundreds up there. So, all the publicity was still only about up there.

Then the owner of Cedar Springs Marina on the far opposite lower end of the reservoir near the dam and outlet phoned me, literally begging me to come down in his area and get him some publicity too because nobody was fishing on that end of the lake.

So, I went down to his marina and started trolling along the shorelines, but only caught very small rainbows... for ten long miles. I wasn't at all impressed by that end of the lake.

Then suddenly I caught a 26 lb. giant trophy brown trout. I kept fishing back and forth right where it had bitten and unbelievably caught a dozen more... all 18-27 lbs. completely unheard of anywhere in the world ever in fishing history for such large brown trout.

I only fished there from then on for all the following years. There was a mountainside of high thick bushes extending under the water with a spring of water flowing into the lake, on a goose neck bend with wind blowing from both directions into that bushes' spring half block long shoreline which all attracted a huge school of chub minnow bait fish to feed there every day then the big trophy fish fed on them.

I noticed what looked like a big hole under a huge boulder on the bank… which became my "cave" I slept in for many years from then on; and that spot became known as "Ray's Cave, Bushes and Gooseneck Bend," where I took all the national magazines and TV stations.

Years later Twitchell reported catching a lake trout, mackinaw up the middle lake at Lucerne, though that species wasn't supposed to be in that lake.

Then another angler reported catching the second confirmed lake trout out of the lake down near the dam.

Next, I caught only the third lake trout I had ever heard of being taken from the lake… while fishing at my bushes by my cave. I soon caught a few more there.

Then an eruption occurred the next year when I caught more than 600 lake trout at my cave where I had only caught big browns, rainbows, and cutthroats all the years before. Obviously large schools of lakers had migrated down the lake and found my huge school of minnow chubs on which to feed.

There weren't supposed to be any lake trout in that reservoir. It was believed that somebody either illegally planted them or else that they migrated down the upper Green River from small lakes in the Wind River Wilderness, some of which do have lake trout in them.

However, a guy who transported fish for planting into various Wyoming Lakes claimed to me that he planted a whole hatchery truck full of little lakers into Flaming Gorge years before which he was supposed to dump into Teton National Park lakes.

Wherever they did originate, all of a sudden there were an awfully lot of them in the lake eating all of the chubs and rainbows and kokanees forage fish crashing the browns' food supply. After famous TV sportscaster Paul James caught lots of big fish with me at both The Gorge and Strawberry, and aired many nights footage for weeks of us catching them… he then asked me if I thought I could catch a record with him in the boat to show him how I went about documenting so many world and state records.

I told him, "Sure thing!" I told him I could catch the new world record lake trout on 4 lb. test line… "on my first cast," not even trolling. "Naw," neither he, his son, nor the cameraman believed that.

We went out over the laker spawning bed in his boat, at The Gorge. I told them they could fish as long as they wanted with whatever they wanted and guaranteed they wouldn't catch any fish no matter how hard they tried.

They tried for hours but didn't catch any fish.

Then they egged me on to prove I could. So, I said, "I'm picking up my magic wand (rod) now. I'm letting my lure sink to the bottom, now I'm reeling it up"… only one, two, three turns of the reel handle and I said, "I've got him"… and jerked.

"No way," they all said… even though my fishing pole was bent double throbbing wildly. They said I just snagged our anchor.

The line was being stripped off my reel extremely fast. Four hours later it became night and dark. It was snowing and wind blowing fiercely cold. Both the big boat engine and the little trolling motor ran out of gas and the boat light batteries and all our flashlight batteries ran down, so we no longer had any light.

They were positive I couldn't ever land that fish on such thin 4 lb. line. They started bribing me with $50.00 and later raised the bribe to $600.00 if I would cut my line and let them flag a boat to take us to shore.

I assured them I could and would land it. Finally, I got it up to the surface. When they saw it in the camera light, they all exclaimed, "It is the world record"… a huge 49-inch-long male lake trout just a smidgen under 50 lbs.

Outdoor Life Magazine writer Jim Zumbo told me he was very skeptical so he wanted to fish with me to see for himself if any of it was true. In his own words: Ray sped us over the water at break neck speed in total darkness well before dawn. I couldn't see a thing and could not understand how he knew where he was. Suddenly he stopped the boat and told me I would catch a big brown right here. In less than a minute I caught the biggest trout of my life…

then several others before it even got light. He proved himself genuine without leaving any doubt!

Jim Zumbo is the national writer who coined the phrase "Hermit of Flaming Gorge" with a beautiful full page cover photo of me sitting in my cave on the cover of *Outdoor Life*. That nickname has been used by many other writers since.

When little I liked to dress up like a cowboy. On one of our family reunions up at Hobble Creek Canyon, I was sitting on a corral fence pretending to ride a horse (the fence) when I fell off into the manure in the corral, covering myself with the smelly stuff.

I waded out in the creek to wash it all off... and noticed lots of brown trout swimming in the water. I went and got my little fishing pole and one of my first lure inventions out of our car... and caught enough trout for everyone to eat.

When we first made my lures by injection molding at Ryder Plastics, they told me everything I wanted to do was impossible and too expensive.

So, I helped machine the expensive hard metal molds the way I wanted (against their wishes).

It worked. My wife Joyce and I took the very first lures shot in the mold that same day down to Utah Lake in the current behind Geneva Steel Mill...and caught dozens of white bass on them.

The next day we took my boat to Strawberry Reservoir and caught more than 200 cutthroat and rainbow trout on them, trolling (pulling them behind the boat).

A short time later the owners of Arctic Star Lodge in Canada invited us (all expenses paid-free) to fly up and fish with them on Great Slave Lake.

During the ten days there, we caught so many fish on my newly invented lures that the owners fed all the guests and staff with them (lake trout, northern pike and grayling).

Our guide took us by boat way far from the lodge to a famous grayling river. On the way he saw and killed a moose, cut it up, and detoured to his cabin to hang it up in his meat shed.

Then he finally continued toward the distant river. When we finally arrived, the water was so clear we could see all the fish swimming out there.

The guide said only one or two could be caught most trips because they were too smart to bite. I caught all 42 of them, putting them into a small pool in the boulders until we were done filming... then released them back into the river. The guide was amazed at my new lures.

Later, on the Great Lakes, I fished with more than fifty different boats... many guides, outfitters, and big lure companies. Every single trip I caught more fish on my lures than they did fishing right next to me with their lures they always used, on their own boats in their home waters.

One famous charter boat captain invited me to fish with him out of Benton Harbor on Lake Michigan. We met before daylight in a cafe for breakfast.

He told me not to expect to catch nearly as many fish as he and his crew would that day, because it was his home port where he fished out of every day... and he knew how to catch them.

A TV station filming crew and a national magazine reporter were both there to document it all.

I told him I didn't want to sound disrespectful like I was bragging, but I said: "This is what is going to happen today in your boat in your home water... I am going to catch all the fish or at least most of them, more than you and your crew... and there is nothing you will be able to do to stop me!"

They all told me I just stuck my neck out farther to be chopped off and humiliated than anyone they had ever met.

Result: That day I caught 65 fish of all sorts of species... trolling with them in their big boat... while they caught none (until late evening and then only a couple of little ones). The fish clearly liked my lures much better than all of theirs.

I had used only two fishing rods and lures and had one of their mates help me reel my fish in. While they used a dozen lines and lures at a time with downriggers, flat lines, planner boards plus outriggers... changing their lures trying different ones constantly, in vain. They were all stunned, couldn't believe their own eyes.

I heard reports from friends and news stories that occasional Tiger Muskies were being caught from Utah's Pineview Reservoir where fishery officials had planted them. So, our family drove up there to check it out.

As it dawned daylight we could see, from high above the lake as we drove around, its big fish, with the tips of their tails and dorsal fins sticking out of the calm surface... which were clearly much longer than just carp.

We parked at a pull-off where the most fish were on the surface and walked down to the shore with our fishing poles.

We soon wondered why we hadn't been fishing there before for years, because we quickly caught nine big long Tiger Muskies.

We fished there a lot often after that, catching first dozens then scores of the Tigers. We have hours of video of my children and wife catching them. We soon also caught the official world record and Utah state record.

We have had much better success casting my lure off the shore banks than trolling or casting from boats. The predatory fish cruise the shorelines and trap the baitfish up against the bank where they can't escape. We often see the little fish flip right out of the water up onto the dry ground trying to get away. We always use double low visibility monofilament, not wire leaders.

We have caught a great many more on the two-inch size of my lure than on any larger sizes. The lake is full of small dollar-sized baitfish, crappies, bluegills and yellow perch which they are used to eating.

The same is true at Flaming Gorge where we catch all of our huge lake trout on my two-inch sized lure, even all of our 50+ pounders (but there from boats, not shore).

They are used to eating baby fingerling kokanee salmon and rainbows and chubs and also crayfish. Also, they will nearly always grab my little 2 incher if it goes in front of their nose for a snack even when they aren't hungry enough to eat a bigger lure or fish.

One same day standing in one same spot on the shoreline of Pineview Reservoir at a place called "Ray's Point" while filming with Utah State University Extension Service casting my little 2 inch size lure off the bank, I caught seventy two fish, one after the other fast... every different species in the lake:

big tiger muskies; brown trout; rainbow trout; cutthroat trout; channel catfish; black bullhead catfish; carp (which don't usually bite on lures); crappie; yellow perch; blue gills; largemouth bass; and small mouth bass.

I have also filmed my children catching all of those many different species there.

At first while fishing for catching the famous trophy brown trout I always used a bare finger on the line to immediately feel the strikes when they bit, grabbed my lure... which was often extremely painful in the bitter cold.

So, I thought of, invented, and started using a rubber band on my line attached to the boat to hook the fish without having to hold my rod pole at all. When fish grab my lure in their mouth, the rubber band stretches only so much before it breaks... hooking the fish without the angler jerking, setting the hook. A catch phrase soon developed: "don't be a jerk," and using rubber bands quickly became famous from national magazine articles about me all across the nation. Now rubber bands are sold in all fishing supply stores everywhere.

I also helped popularize the use of rubber bands all across the Great Lakes, while fishing with hundreds of other boats there.

Another groundbreaking invention I developed starting when I was 5 years old was making a "hole" in each of my lures. Why? I put some kind of bait or scent into it to help attract fish to bite better than on an unscented lure alone.

I put a piece of fish skin or meat or other bait in the hole to create a scent trail in the water to help attract fish to try and eat my lure. Otherwise, I put a small piece of red felt in the hole to hold any liquid or paste scent longer from being quickly washed away... a "meat pocket" and "scent pocket."

Throughout the years, this changed the fishing lure industry developing into universal use amongst lure manufacturers. A little hole in lures and a little rubber band I invented changed the entire fishing world (along with trolling at night in darkness).

I have always preferred small lengths, short rubber bands, because they stretch less so hook fish quicker. Many other people use much longer bands because they are easier to tie... put around the line then through itself and pulled tightly cinched on the line... the other end of the band hooked attached to an s-bent wire or other clamping device on the boat, downrigger, or out-rigger, or planer board. That enables the rod to be put and kept into a rod holder on the edge of the boat so it doesn't have to be held by the angler.

I always cinch a couple of extra bands, next to the first one to keep the line from slipping through it, cut off short so they will easily reel through the rod's guides and onto the reel, as "stoppers." If the line slips through them the fish when it bites won't get hooked as well, or not at all.

There is an important technical difference in the use of the cut-off stopper bands. When using a flat or shallow line trolling the stopper bands need to be cinched "below" the hooking band to keep the line from slipping through when pulled tight by a fish (toward the lure).

But just the opposite, they need to be placed on the line "above" it when fishing any depths below the surface... to keep the water pressure from pulling the lure closer to the boat or downrigger.

At deep depths I place stopper bands both "above" and "below" the hooking band to prevent line slippage from both water pressure and a hard strike.

I have always used "genuine rubber" bands, not synthetic plastic ones which are much too strong to break on a strike. These are just a few of the many things I have invented and originated which have been widely adopted and used over much of the world. I also use rubber bands on my downrigger wire cable to stack multiple lines at different levels.

The first thing before you can catch fish you have to find them, exactly pinpoint them, and put your hook right in front of their nose. Fish finders and underwater cameras are universally used these days. But I used none of them back in the earlier times catching the trophy browns.

Also, today anglers are allowed to use two or more multiple lines per person. Utah only allowed one line during most of my trophy catch years.

Once the fish are found, I always mark them precisely with lines attached to floating markers on the surface and heavy weights on the line's other end down on the lake's bottom, to keep wind and waves from drifting the markers away.

Then I troll my boat close back and forth past the markers downwind so I don't snag their line.

But other anglers also see my markers and crowd around me, so I invented decoy "seagull" ones from a mold I made from a dead one. Painted realistically which look alive just like live birds floating on the water's surface. Seagulls live everywhere around water and most anglers don't even notice mine aren't real.

When necessary, I decoy the other anglers away from where I really am catching my fish by placing big highly visible square Styrofoam markers a little distance away from my seagull ones.

I invented the use of large heavy hourglass shaped rubber boat trailer rollers to use as my marker weights. I pour one with its end into the bottom of each seagull marker to ride the seagull upright on the waves and attach the line to. Then I wrap the other end of the line around another heavy roller long enough to reach the lake's bottom.

When I throw one out on the water, the roller weight cleanly unwinds the line wrapped around it all the way down to the lake bottom without tangling. Its heavy weight keeps the wind and waves from unwinding any slack line drifting the seagull above away.

I retrieve it back by winding the line around the roller stuck out of the seagull marker. To use again, I rewrap the line all around the weight roller.

I also invented 12 lb. heavy fish-shaped downrigger weights covered with a realistic flexible coating with waving fins and tail, just like my fish lure... which attract fish to come look at them closely instead of scaring them away like most other downrigger weights.

I don't like lighter weights less than 12 lbs. because they don't go straight enough down without angling back behind the boat from the moving water pressure. You can only know your lure's true depth if the weight stays straight down.

Because fly fishing is so popular, I also invented a fly we have caught numerous official world records on of a few species (many fish eat insects, of course).

Jigs are a universally popular lure to catch many species of fish. I invented my "Whoopie Fly" to dazzle national magazines and TV stations and critics. It is merely a "bare hook" with a small split shot sinker at its loop top... no feathers, no plastic, no bait.

Many fish try to eat it just because I jump it and let it fall repeatedly, much to the utter amazement of those I show it to... catching fish on a bare, bait-less hook.

My kids also created a sensation that has now lasted for many years catching the spawning rainbow trout in the Spring on the Lucerne Marina boat ramp with their fly rods.

While trolling for kokanee salmon with my lures, my little daughter Lisa caught a huge 49 lb. lake trout which took her forever to reel in, it fought so hard. It was almost as long as she was tall. She couldn't lift it up nor hardly hold it on her lap while I videoed it.

We released it, and the Wyoming Fish Wardens asked if they could take our camera to show the video to some others.

When they brought it back to us, Lisa was just catching a big 35 lb. laker on her fly rod fishing for the spawning rainbows on the Lucerne Marina concrete boat ramp.

The rumor started and spread widely that it was the 49 pounder she caught on her flyrod on the boat ramp. I still hear people believe that today.

She, Lisa, later held the most official both world and state fish records of all women in history in the world. And my youngest son, Kirk, held the most world and state records of all men in the world, except me.

In 1985 I, Ray Johnson, was inducted into the Fishing Hall of Fame.

My children have also caught much publicized world and state records. Examples:

- 178 Total Combined Official World and State Records
- 137 Total World Records
- 41 Total State Records
- 107 Total Hall of Fame World Records
- 30 Total International Game Fish Association World Records

Official Utah State Lake Trout Records Released Alive:

- 39 ¼ May 3, 1997 eight-year-old Kirk Ray Johnson

- 40 ½ inches May 10, 1997 six-year-old Lisa Johnson
- 41 inches July 4, 1997 eight-year-old Kirk Ray Johnson
- 41 ½ inches (51 lb. 12 oz.) July 5, 1997 six-year-old Lisa Johnson
- 45 inches (51 lb. 14 oz.) July 11, 1997 eight-year-old Kirk Ray Johnson
- 46 ½ inches (52 lb. 1 oz) July 9, 1998 Ray Johnson
- 49 inches (49 lb. 14 oz.) May 1997 six-year-old Lisa Johnson in Wyoming

Note: Wyoming State did not keep released State Records

- 48 inches (51 lb. 10 oz.) Ray Johnson
- 49 inches (49 lb. 14 oz.) Ray Johnson

Note: These both caught before Utah started its Release Program
Note: Official both World and Utah State Tiger Muskellunge Released Record

- 53 ¼ inches November 28, 1998 Ray Johnson
- 26 ⅝ inches May 29, 2004 Ray Johnson

Note: Official both World and Utah State Kokanee Salmon Released Record

Links to Videos and Other Documents
1. Ray Johnson Documentary:
   https://www.youtube.come/watch?v=9E8Wblqz1Sc
2. Fishing Flaming Gorge:
   https://www.youtube.com/watch?v=P2mkSZXRGns
3. Filming Documentary of Ray Johnson:
   https://www.youtube.com/watch?v=t0Lakceqaa8
7. Kirk Johnson reading the Hall of Fame Plaque:
   https://youtube.com/watchv=zSOXRTE9bil
8. Hall of Fame Plaque:
   https://www.youtube.com/watch?v=WuOyTUikFfs

9. Ray's lure is what makes him a great fisherman:
    https://www.youtube.com/watchv=eWVzBRxi9gw

10. How to catch big fish:
    https://www.youtube.come/watch?v=hZ4UVzk5Cwy

11. Utah's most famous angler:
    https://www.ksl.com/index.php?sid=27320413&nid=481

12. Photo of Ray with lunker trout:
    https://www.ksl.com/?sid=27320143

13. Utah State fishing records:
    https://wildlife.utah.gov/record-fish.html

14. Book Review: *Big Trout*
    https:www.lakeontariounited.com/fishing hunting/topic/48594-book-re-
    view/big-trout-by-ray-johnson/

15. Best fisherman in the History of the World:
    https://www.facebook.com/notes/primal chase/best-fisherman-in-the-his-
    tory-of-the-world-2006/430907270298195/

More Search Words/ links

1. Ray Johnson fisherman

3. Real minnow lure

5. Utah.boy37@yahoo.com

6. (info) 435-200-LURE

7. www.ksl.com ?sid=273204138nid=utahrsguos-most-famous-angler-still-
    catching-lunkers-after- 60-years&fm=home pagee8s cid=queue-4 Enter
    keyword all of KSL Utah's most famous angler still catching lunkers after
    60 years ksl.com

8. www.sportsmanwarehouse.com Real minnow lure. Ray Johnson's lure.

9. Utah's own captain Ahab. Moby dick. Salt lake tribune.

10. *People Magazine*. Ray Johnson angler

11. *Sports Afield Magazine*. Ray Johnson fisherman.

12. *Outdoor Life Magazine*. Hermit of flaming gorge.

13. Oct. 25, 2013 Flaming Gorge National Recreation Area- Ray Johnson is

Utah's most famous angler. He's been inducted into the Fresh Water Fishing Hall of Fame, holds multiple state and world records.

14. Dec. 12, 2015 Ray Johnson Documentary- YouTube.

Sources of quotes in Fishing Hall of Fame Display

- "He is the world's greatest trout angler." *People Magazine*, March 30, 1981
- "As far as we know, Ray (Johnson) was the first angler ever in *People Magazine*." Bill Shaw

●●

Quotes from Fishing Hall of Fame, Vol. 9 No. 2, 1985
- "North America's greatest angler?" (If you don't think so, Prove it!)
- "He unlocked a secret he since has shared with the world freely."
- "His Real Minnow Lure is the key to his success."
- "Too few market writers and industry people have fished with him and his lure... his philosophy is that fishing is for fun and sport, not monetary gain."
- "Ray Johnson is a Hall of Fame Legendary Angler which honor is more than well justified."
- "It would be interesting to see his 'Real Minnow' technique put the bass experts on alert.
- "The 'legend of Ray Johnson' prevails."

●●

Quotes from Cover Story from *Sports Afield*, February 1976, LaMar Underwood, Editor
- "Read how this man catches more trout over ten pounds from public water than any angler in history!"

- Ray Johnson proves that the world of angling is still full of wonder and surprise for the man who is willing to dare to be a little different."
- "He has enjoyed fishing success for brown, rainbow, cutthroat, and lake trout of sizes unheard of and unequaled in any time and place in history, from easily accessible hard-fished public water."
- "He has caught trout of each of all four species over 10 lbs. 'the same day' many times."

● ●

Quotes from Carl Malz and Spence Petros.
Fishing Facts, February 1977

- "Extremely hardworking super-trout expert RAY JOHNSON is creating 'tremors in the fishing fraternity' with his world record catches, amazing the best experts, capturing more large trout from public waters than any other angler in history."
- "He has been able to capture giant, trophy, and record class fish from waters which stump a majority of other anglers. His secret? His lure! Because a great many fish recognize the 'phoniness' of most lures and refuse to strike them"
- "Ray's giant catches have 'rocked much of the fishing world and created a great deal of excitement among thousands of anglers.'"
- "The fact that one person has managed to catch so many more fish and larger fish than all the rest of the anglers trying combined, is a clear indication that it is possible to do something drastically different than everyone else does and, thereby, enjoy far greater success."
- "He does the many little 'insignificant things,' which put all together make a BIG difference. There are larger fish in most waters than are being caught by most anglers, but it is possible to learn to catch them, as Ray constantly proves."

● ●

Quotes from Hartt Wixom,

Argosy, May 1978

- "The other great names in angling, from Izaac Walton to A.J. Mclane, would have been proud of Ray Johnson's accomplishments… legendary sizes of fish by any legal method of capture."
- "No angler in modern history, to our knowledge, has caught as many brown trout over 10 pounds, or over 20 pounds as has Johnson." (As far as we know, Ray was the first angler ever featured in Argosy.)

••

Quote from Rex Thomas,

Fins & Feathers, **1984**

- "Ray has caught more trophy class trout than any other living fisherman. It took Johnson to prove the rest of the world wrong about fishing. His perfected fishing skills and wealth of knowledge make all things possible."

••

Quotes from Matt Vincent.

The *IN-FISHERMAN*, February 1989

- "Ray Johnson is the 'king' of world fishing records and the world's best fisherman! He has caught more record-size fish of different species and more big trout from public waters than anyone living and than anybody in history!"
- "The publicity and articles written about him in most outdoor magazines as well as in others like People Magazine, Reader's Digest, and Argosy would make a patch-covered bass fisherman green with envy."
- "He has caught more larger brown, rainbow, cutthroat, and lake trout from public water than any other angler in history."

●●

Quotes from Craig LaRocco.

Fins and Feathers. **Winter Special Edition, 1986**

- "World- renowned angler RAY JOHNSON has caught literally thousands of rainbows, lake trout, cutthroats, and brown trout weighing well over 10 pounds each... my first trout fishing with him was a 25-pounder and my next even larger."

- "As his list of accomplishments and his reputation continue to grow, rumors claiming he employs illegal methods to catch his fish are surfacing. Nothing could be further from the truth."

- Surprisingly, he uses the same lure and the same technique for ALL FISH! 'Real Minnow Lures' of his own design and manufacture... and markers to pinpoint fish, to keep his lure in quality water in front of fish constantly all the time."

- "I have caught and I know many other anglers who have caught as many as 60 lake trout in a single day with Ray at Flaming Gorge at slow times of the year when other fishermen catch none or a few and say they can only be caught then with luck."

- "He is the best because he puts a lot of work into it, he says (but somehow, catching huge fish and breaking record after record just doesn't sound like work)."

●●

Quote from Tom Hardin.

Action Fishing, **1982**

- "Year in and year out, Johnson is 'by far' the most successful trophy trout fisherman, perhaps because of his special lure which he manufactures."

●●

Quote from Michael Rutter.

Western Outdoors, **September 1986**

- "When it comes to big fish, few names are as impressive as Ray Johnson's. He became famous in the early '70s when he was pronounced the world's greatest brown trout fisherman by outdoor writers. And the momentum hasn't stopped yet."

••

Quotes from Bill Shaw.

Western Outdoors, **February 1983**

- "Ray Johnson catches fish like no man before him. He is the world's greatest fisherman. He is a living legend. He is a hero, a modern-day legend."
- "There is a clamor for the artificial lures he makes for himself."
- "Ray Johnson, known as the 'Hermit of Flaming Gorge,' is the world's greatest fisherman."

••

Quotes from Flaming Gorge Fishing Map

Angler's Inn. Flaming Gorge, Utah, 1976 (over 120,000 copies sold)

- "Ray's lures are the very best invented, the most realistic and effective of all lures. They make other lures obsolete!"

••

Quote from Fishing Hall of Fame *SPLASH*, 1985

- "There is no question that Ray Johnson is a living legend. Virtually all of the major fishing and outdoor publications have certified his credibility by sending writers along as fishing companions on one or more of Ray's safaris... where they have witnessed Ray's unusual tactics which have yielded for him more brown trout over 20 pounds than have been taken by any other man in history."

••

Quotes from Mike Ratter.

Midwest Outdoors/Western Outdoors, **September 1983**

- "Last month I had the opportunity to get a world famous celebrity out on Lake Michigan- Ray Johnson, better known as the 'Hermit of Flaming Gorge'- who proved to be one of the most interesting, colorful, and knowledgeable fishing personalities I have ever met. His unique personality and fishing accomplishments have made him known throughout the world.

- "He is said by many to be "THE WORLD'S GREATEST FISHER-MAN." I am sure you will find him as fascinating as I did. No nonsense! He really does have and use new, different methods (some secret) that will catch you more fish too."

••

Quotes from Bob Swirz, Editor,
Fishing Annual/Guide, December 1978

- "I am featuring Ray Johnson's new 'Real Minnow Lures' in no less than six different articles in this issue because I have never had such good immediate success for so large nor so many fish with any new lure."

- "I caught by far my three biggest brown trout ever the first day. I have fished for weakfish in the Salt all my life, ever since I was growing up, but never caught so many so big in such a short time as I just did on his lure. I am going to do a lot more fishing with them. I think they are great!"

- "He caught a 25 lb. male brown 'twice' the same day."

●●

Quotes from Jim Zumbo.
Outdoor Life **Fishing Annual, 1987**

- "It wasn't until I met Ray Johnson that I learned fishing's peculiarities. He was well known then, and for good reason. But I was skeptical. I needed to know if he was on the level (so I fished with him.)."

- "It didn't take long for me to become convinced that Johnson was genuine, though. He tore us along in the dark in his boat at breakneck speed. I couldn't see a thing. Suddenly he stopped and told me I would get a strike on one of his lures right 'here' within a minute or two."

- "(I still couldn't see a thing and can't understand how he could possibly know where he was.) In less than a minute I felt a solid strike and battled the largest brown trout of my life to the boat."

- "I was absolutely amazed. We boated a good number of other browns and I gained a new respect for the man before it even got daylight. He indeed knew what he was doing."

●●

Quotes from Bob Zwirz, Editor,
Fishing and Boating Guide, 1978

- "The new 'Real Minnow Lure' brought out by Ray Johnson, is as deadly as any lure I've fished yet. Fish simply engulf them. It has already produced as many fish as any lure I have ever used."

- "[Ray Johnson's 'Real Minnow Lure' is] the most realistic, best working plug-type lure and [has the most fish-alluring fantastic wiggle of any lure available.]"

●●

Quotes from Mike Simmons,
Sports Week/ Outdoor Cabin Fever Show, April 1983

- "The highlight of the Cabin Fever Show this year will no doubt be Ray Johnson and his lure and his book... Outdoor Life, Sports Afield. People Magazine and others have credited him with catching more large trout over 20 lbs. than anyone in angling history."
- "Ray's fame is a result of his fishing successes with his own fishing lure he invented. The appearance of nationally famous Ray Johnson at this year's show is an example of the growth in stature of this annual sportsman's Great Lakes event."

•••

Quotes from Gus Brannon,
Nevada Fishing News, 1984

- "I get very skeptical about supposed 'miracle baits.' After a thorough testing, however, all I can say about Ray Johnson's 'Real Minnow Lures' is that 'they out-fish and out-catch' all of my pet baits on Pyramid Lake, here in Nevada. This is not speculation, but having one bait on a downrigger and a 'Real Minnow Lure' on the other at the same depth at the same time."
- "Virtually all of the largest fish have come on the 'Real Minnow Lure.' The first few times I used them I thought it might be that the lures were just on the 'hot rods' those particular days. But now, after all these times with the same thing always happening, and after so many big fish, it just simply can't be."
- "I never thought there could be that much difference between lures. One day we caught fish so fast we couldn't keep the line with the 'Real Minnow Lure' in the water for hours. None of the other lures on any of the other rods caught any fish that day at all."

•••

Miscellaneous Short Quotes

- "Ray Johnson, known as the 'HERMIT' of Flaming Gorge, is the 'World's Greatest Fisherman!'" <u>The Chicago Tribune. 1981</u>
- "Ray Johnson has shocked the fishing world and single-handedly turned it upside down like a number 8 earthquake on the Richter Scale." <u>Normark Fishing Guide Book. 1976</u>
- "Ray Johnson Shattered the national fishing establishment, like a Number Eight quake on the Richter Scale." <u>Normark Fishing Guide Book. 1977</u>

●●

Quotes from Rex Thomas,
Rocky Mountain Sportsman, July 1986

- "He is the most famous trophy trout fisherman."
- "He has boated hundreds of brown trout and lake trout over 20 lbs. each."
- "I was speechless as Ray released my first trout, a 21-pounder, assuring me I would catch a larger one. He was right. Just 15 minutes later I caught a 26 pound trout on his Real Minnow lure... Many days he catches over 300 lbs. of trout in a single day!"
- "I quickly learned how little I really knew about fishing, even though I have been at it over 30 years... and learned how extremely knowledgeable Ray Johnson is about all kinds of fishing."
- "He and his fishing and his lure are all unlike any you have ever known."
- "After studying Johnson and his lure and method and fishing with him over 20 days, I can tell you that luck has little, if anything, to do with his success. He has taken knowledge- a vast amount of hard-earned knowledge - and then refined his fishing skills to a science where he can very accurately predict where the fish will be and how many and what sizes he will catch each day."

- "The best way for other anglers to learn how to catch trophy fish is for them to take a closer look at how 'the expert' Ray Johnson does it. He only uses ONE LURE- his Real Minnow Lure. Every little compartment in his tackle box is crammed with them... I strongly suggest you all try them... he developed a better lure the likes of which you have never seen before... which really entices all kinds of game fish."

● ●

Quotes from *Fins and Feathers*,
September 1985

- "Ray Johnson is honored in a very big way by just being inducted into the NATIONAL FRESH WATER FISHING HALL OF FAME as a legendary angler, the only Utahn and one of only a very few living anglers ever so honored."
- "Both the International Game Fish Association and The Fishing Hall of Fame credit Johnson with having caught more line-class game fish world records than any other person in history."
- "Ray also holds more approved 'state record' fish than any other angler ever."

● ●

Quote from Hartt Wixom.
***Utah Outdoors*, May 1978**

- "I just spent one week with Ray Johnson to see how he catches so many large trout. His unorthodox techniques have caught for this unique angler more large trout in just two years probably than anyone in the history of the sport has ever caught in their entire life (to say nothing about all the other years Ray fished and will yet fish)."
- "I've also learned they are excellent lures for most other species of game fish."

• •

Quotes from David Richey,
Detroit News, **1986**

- "Within minutes Johnson was into a king... and then Johnson hooked another, and another. My lures were losers... before I could swallow my pride and ask for a lure. A big chinook nailed it immediately."
- "I'm convinced something exciting and new has come to Lake Michigan in this new lure. Not many anglers caught 'any' kings that day."

• •

Quote from Bill Shaw.
People Magazine. Chicago Tribune **Special, 1981**

- "Ray Johnson is indisputably the best angler in the world- THE WORLD'S GREATEST FISHERMAN! 34-year-old Ray Johnson is a living legend, a hero... the world's greatest fisherman."

• •

Quote from Lee Nelson.
Utah Journal, **1985**

- "Bill Shaw and People Magazine were NOT EXAGGERATING when they called Ray Johnson 'the best fisherman in the world.' I saw for myself. All of his fish are caught on the same lure- the 'Real Minnow' which looks, feels, and wiggles like a baby fish (with a huge treble hook attached to the belly)."
- "By mid-afternoon we had caught over 20 lake trout. Suddenly I realized why Ray ruins lots of marriages. I was trying to figure out how to convince my wife that we needed to invest in a boat, motor, downriggers, fish finder, truck to pull it, and camper to stay in, etc."

- "World famous Ray Johnson [is] undeniably the WORLD'S GREATEST LIVING FISHERMAN!"

••

Quotes from the Editors of *Sports Afield*,
April 1976

- "Unbelievable! We just ran a feature story about Ray Johnson in our recent February issue of <u>Sports Afield</u> about the mammoth brown trout he has been catching in Flaming Gorge Reservoir, and he has just caught another, this one a 29-1/2 pounder that is also the new six-pound test world record, beating the old record by eight pounds."
- "No one has had the experience of landing the numbers of large trout he has had. It should be very interesting to see what develops with him in the future. We will keep close tabs on him."

••

Quotes from Tom Huggler.
Bass and Freshwater Fishing Annual.
***Outdoor Life*, 1987**

- "Here's the advice of a real specialist, who can catch trophy browns when no one else can get a hit."
- "No story on huge brown trout would be complete without mentioning Ray Johnson... who has perhaps caught more trophy fish than anyone else in the world!"
- "He uses his Real Minnow Lures which he makes himself."

••

**Quote from *Western Outdoors*,
August 1976**

- "Ray Johnson has enticed far more trophy fish from the water than any other fisherman ever in history. He is truly a legendary angler."

••

**Quotes from Rex Thomas,
Petersen's Fishing,
January 1989 and March 1989
(two-parter)**

- "Famous fisherman Ray Johnson is the 'key' to learning to use downriggers, and to learning a lot more. The most interesting downrigger weight I have ever seen is Ray Johnson's own designed "fish" weight- a fish look-alike that actually has flexible, movable fins and tail, etc., and attracts fish instead of scaring them like all other cannonballs. One reason his catch rate is so greatly improved over even professional guides."
- "Another [reason his catch rate is so good) is the many versatile ways he uses rubber bands to hook fish. His all-consuming constant use of markers to keep fish located is another. But his own designed Real Minnow Lure is the biggest reason he catches so many fish."

••

**Quotes from Joe Dennis,
Fishing Hunting News, January 1979**

- "Master angler Ray Johnson has made Flaming Gorge Reservoir synonymous with heaven for trout fisherman the world over. His credentials are impeccable."
- "His 'Real Minnow lure' is effective because it presents a realistic baitfish to the fish, with tail and fins, etc."

- "Last week he again set still a new record for brown trout on a six-pound test line. Following Fishing & Hunting News will offer some tips from Johnson on how to hook husky Mackinaw (lake trout) over 30 lbs."

• •

Quotes from Tom Hardin
Action Fishing Annual, 1982

- "Year in and year out, Ray Johnson is by far the most successful trophy trout fisherman at Flaming Gorge. His success is so great that hordes of other anglers follow him wherever he goes to fish by him and his markers."
- "Perhaps his secret is in his own special lure he uses."

• •

Quote from the Editor of
Mid-West Outdoors, **1979**

- "Many anglers think so highly of Ray Johnson that they will travel across continents just to fish with him."

• •

Quotes from Charles Davis.
Fishing and Hunting News,
September 1978

- "NEW MINNOW LURE PASSES TEST! I met Ray Johnson at AFTMA's extravaganza show. He has been written up in many national magazines because of his expertise in catching 'LARGE' trout and other fish on his own designed lure, the 'Real Minnow.'"
- "In looking at the bait, it really does look like a fish from every angle. The detail is realistic even close up. He makes it out of a rubber-like plastic, molded in the shape of a minnow (it looks like a sculpin to

me) with great detail of scales and fins. It even has a movable tail."

- "The built-in lip gives the bait a rolling and darting action that drives fish to strike. The action of the lure combined with the lifelike appearance is really different than all other lures."
- "The pectoral fins protrude from the body and the dorsal and tail fins give the lure a good silhouette. The detail of the scales, nose, eyes, etc., make even a close-up inspection realistic."

• •

Quotes from Rex Thomas.
***Fins and Feathers*, 1984**
- "Without a doubt the person who has caught the most trophy trout is nationally known Ray Johnson. Fishing with him, even I boated six trout, each over 20 lbs. in weight, in one day."
- "Johnson fishes exclusively with a unique lure he designed, manufactures, and markets- the Real Minnow. I can personally recommend them, having caught all of the largest lakers and browns of my life while using them."

• •

National Fresh Water Fishing Hall of Fame, 1985
- "[Ray Johnson] inducted into the Fishing Hall of Fame." (Coincidentally, the same year as Lauri Rapala was enshrined.)

• •

Jim McCrea, NR Sports, 1984
- "Ray Johnson has caught more large trout than anyone in history. He's the best damn fisherman I have ever seen... He catches all of his fish on his own custom-designed minnow lures."

●●●

Editor, *Fins & Feathers*, 1984

- "Ray Johnson's 'Real Minnow Lures' have proven to be absolutely deadly on Pyramid cutthroats."

●●●

Ray Ostrom and Ron Weber, Normark Corporation, 1976

- "No lure that looks like a fish, has a tail or fins, sells well nor catches fish well!"

Partial List of Magazines, Etc., with Feature Articles (too many other issues, newspaper articles, etc., to list)

Action Fishing

Argosy

Boating & Fishing Annual (many different issues)

Central Utah Journal

Field & Stream

Fins & Feathers

Fishing & Boating Illustrated

Fishing & Hunting News (over 30 separate issues)

Fishing Facts

Fishing Guide to Utah

Mormon World Records- Skousen

The In-Fisherman

International Angler

Midwest Outdoors

Normark Fishing Guide

Outdoor Life (many, many issues)

Pennsylvania Sportsman

People

Rocky Mountain Sportsman

Salmon Unlimited

Splash

Sports Afield (many different issues)

Utah Fins & Feathers

Utah Fishing

Utah Outdoors (in over 20 different issues)

Utah Sportsman News

Walleye Fisherman

Western Outdoors (many separate issues)

Western Outdoors News (many different issues)

Western Outdoorsman

Google Search Results:

Book Review- *Big Trout!* by Ray Johnson- Open Lake Discussion... Lake Ontario United>topic>48594- bo...

Jan 5, 2015. Four posts. Three authors. Was published by Ray Johnson In 1980, distributed by the Peton Corporation. Ray was in his early thirties at the time. He chronicles his fishing adventures in Utah's Flaming Gorge Reservoir...

Ray Johnson- Utah Wildlife Network. Utahwildlife.net>forum>14604-ray-joh...

August 6, 2009. Ray Johnson was/? Is a very colorful and sometimes controversial character. He had an obsession for catching big fish and literally spent a lifetime fishing Flaming Gorge probably at the expense of a...

The Big One That Got Away Is Not A Fish but a Truly Extraordinary Fisherman, Hermit Ray Johnson. People.com>archive>the-big-one-that-...

Ray Johnson artist/Amazon Official Site www.amazon.com/books/art-photography

Mar 30. 1981 Ray Johnson has never been hooked by social conventions.

Ron Weber and Ray Ostrom of famous Lauri Rapala's Normark Lures and knives and Fiskars scissors flew to Utah and fished with me, then flew me and Joyce back to their Minnesota headquarters and made me an offer to manufacture my lures.

They certainly could have sold many millions of my lures as they have done with Rapala Lures. But I wanted a guaranteed lifetime income like their workers who make Rapala Lures in Finland have. So, I didn't accept their one-time buyout payment offer.

They had me develop the "perch color" for their lures. I tried to get them to make my most famous "frog color," but they felt that didn't make sense for a minnow lure. That frog color has become famous now with many brands of lures, like Flatfish Lures.

I originally called my lures "Real Minnows" because of all their fins and pliable waving tail and side fins sticking out away from the lure body, just like a real fish. They later became named "The Legend" because The Hall of Fame and national magazines all called me "A True Living Legend."

Most other plug type and fish shaped lures have always had two or three or more small hooks on them, most missing many fish which bite them or coming unhooked.

So, I invented my huge "anchor-sized hook" much larger per size of lure than all other lures.

I hate missing any fish bite not being hooked or having any hooked fish ever coming unhooked.

My lures securely hook nearly every fish which bites on them and seldom do any come unhooked.

The big treble hook hanging down swinging on my lure's belly also helps create the many erratic wiggles of my lures and waves like fish fins.

I have numerous copyrights on my lures, books and maps.

While trying to hold my World Record and Utah State Record huge 53-inch-long Tiger Musky up for photos and video it jerked its head sideways grabbing my thumb... almost biting it completely off, bleeding profusely.

The very first pass along my cave's bushes the first time I ever used my new injected lures out of the mold on Flaming Gorge I caught a 26-lb. line class world record brown with my uncle Hyrum, then he caught one. He and his family, my cousins, then later caught lots of them... a whole bunch during one night alone. How was that for quick success on my new lures.

I was showing Russ Duket, owner of Cedar Springs Marina, how I caught lots of chubs and rainbows on my "Whoopie" bare hook, when I amazingly caught a 25-lb. brown on it out of the midst of the school of chubs in the little boat dock bay. We filled my aluminum boat completely full with hundreds of chubs we caught for photos.

Paul Marzuaran hooked but lost a big brown while fishing with me breaking his line. The next day we caught and landed that 19-lb. brown with the former day's lure and line still in its mouth.

Utah sports TV broadcaster known and promoted as "Mr. Utah Outdoors" and I caught a huge 20-lb. class brown at my cave on film. He let others know we caught it via ship to shore and CB. Two other news men in another boat farther up the lake wanted to come and see it.

Somehow, they crashed their boat into a cliff curling the front bow of the boat back like Aladdin's shoe. Luckily, they weren't seriously hurt.

I took him, Doug Miller, deer hunting in a grain field up East Canyon. We sat in an old covered wagon for a blind and he shot his biggest buck out of the pioneer wagon on film.

TV sports anchor Steve Brown brought a cameraman and friends to fish with me at my cave. We had good success catching some big trophy browns.

Then I took them a couple miles farther up Red Canyon Gorge in the boat to Carter Creek where rainbow trout were spawning at the inlet... and dazzled them catching lots of the rainbow trout fast on my "Whoopie Fly" (bare hook). They couldn't believe what they were seeing and filming.

Salt Lake Tribune sportswriter Tom Wharton caught an unusually big brook trout fishing with me at Strawberry reservoir, which I got mounted for him, which he displayed on his wall. His cat smelled it and tried to eat it, ruining the taxidermy mount.

He wrote many articles about me over the years and was the one to coin the phrase: "Utah's Own Captain Ahab" in a lengthy multipage story about me. Other writers since have also used his catchy name for me.

Spencer Kinard and Don Judd from a Salt Lake TV station and Ray Reymond from the Fish and Game were surprised at how fast and how close to the boat dock we all caught big browns when they fished and filmed with me.

Another time Don Judd brought a little boy from an orphanage whom I let use my pole, and he caught big fish quickly on film. Don Judd from TV did also.

Almost the entire crew from Channel 4 TV fished with me, and sports anchor Steve Brown caught two browns of 12 and 15 lbs. first, all of them ribbing me about that. But shortly after I caught a 22-lb. female and a 21-lb. male brown on film with their cameramen Bob Innes and Steve Henline.

My close friends Paul Mazuran and George Lelis and I caught an enormous haul of three limits of trophy browns all one night near Buckboard, in the dark.

George and I kept catching all of them quickly while Paul didn't catch any. Then he shined his flashlight on his lure and noticed that it didn't have any hook on it. For a joke we had taken the hook off of his lure on his line. He didn't think that it was funny.

After daylight we took the three limits of 24 big trophy browns to the Buckboard old original store, put them all on a long rope and stretched them across the porch tied on the handrails on both sides. The weight broke both down... what photos that made!

Another friend, Louie Girgudo had his big cabin cruiser boat jump its hitch and break the safety chain going up steep Parley's Canyon.

We saw thousands of fire sparks as its trailer tongue dragged along the asphalt road picking up speed rolling backward a long distance before going off the road into the mountain side.

Another time the same friend drove his big boat right out of the water a long distance from the shore into the sagebrush losing his way in the dark, evidently riding a bow wave other the dry ground.

When he walked clear over to our camp and woke me up, he said, "You will never believe where my boat is!" He took me over there and he was right, I couldn't believe my eyes where his boat was, far from the water's edge, out in the dry ground sagebrush.

When I dropped photographer Dan Bergeron and his friend John Forster off at Cedar Springs after fishing together, we saw a couple of guys with his car trunk open stealing things. They threatened us with a bat when we confronted them.

But Dan had a gun and forced the thief couple to lay face down on the ground in the snow until the sheriff deputies arrived.

For many years Fred Clark let me fish for free in one of his old big wooden rental boats at his boat camp. I would often drive all the way from Salt Lake five evenings a week after my masonry work there to Strawberry Reservoir.

Several boat camps there had photos on their walls of large fish I had caught. Fred liked to eat bottled trout.

Several world record fish mounts plus many dozens of photos are on display at the Fishing Hall of Fame in Hayward, Wisconsin of our family's record fish catches, plus plaques and articles.

Many years after the Flaming Gorge dam was built, water regulator outlets were built on it to take the warmest water out of the lake to warm the Green River water below hoping it would help those fish grow faster and larger.

What resulted was it froze the lake surface over sooner, thicker and longer.

The wind blowing from two directions with the springs at my bushes cave had always kept that lake bend free of ice every winter.

I woke up before dawn to fish one morning, and my boat tied against the shore was frozen in solid ice and the entire lake was frozen, where it had never frozen before. I had to leave my boat and motor and everything else there for three months, until the Spring thaw, and hike 2,000 feet up the steep mountainside in the snow and walk several more miles out to the road and hitch hike 200 miles to get home.

Quite a few deer walk out on the ice when parts of the lake are frozen over at the Gorge slipping and, sliding and unable to run, are caught and eaten by coyotes.

A neighbor fell through the lake ice on his snowmobile while ice fishing nearly drowning... other anglers also.

A guy drove his truck on the snow and ice too close to the water on the shore right in front of our boat. His vehicle slid into the lake and sunk below the surface, the engine still running briefly creating bubbles. We rescued him in my boat.

While trolling deep, we accidently snagged a rope, pulled it up attached to a canoe some people had sunk in windy waves and drowned in, retrieving it all to the surface.

I caught a huge 26-lb. brown at Gold Point with Mr. and Mrs. Miller. As I released it trying to hold it for photos, it flopped hard out of my hands back into the water breaking my line with the lure still in its mouth, losing my lure.

Incredibly, later that day while again fishing in that same spot, I caught that same huge trophy fish again. Even more remarkably, my hook wasn't even stuck in its mouth, but only the hook prong on my lure on my line was hooked around a prong of the lost lure in its mouth.

John Savage of Savage Glass was a fervent critic of me, so I invited him fishing. He had never caught any big brown trout. He wanted us to fish in his boat. Within minutes in the dark before daylight at Buckboard's Big Bend point trolling, I caught a big trophy brown. Shortly after I caught another even bigger one.

He caught none because his boat wiring caught on fire and he was busy trying to keep his boat from burning. I then caught a third.

Later I invited him to show him my famous "Bushes" spot by my cave where I caught most of my largest trophy browns. He brought his own boat with friends to meet me there... but came just a little too late. I had already caught a 27-lb. or so huge brown and was holding it in the water until they came to show it to them before releasing it.

They begged me to give it to them. I told them they could keep it if they could catch it in their net when I threw it over the water... and they did. Nobody gives such a huge brown away. With my published book *Big Trout*, I included everyone else I was aware of who had caught big fish from the lake.

I usually caught a trophy brown close to or over 20 lbs. at least every three days or less. Not many times but a few times one of the big fish has grabbed two of our lures on different lines and been caught on both at the same time.

With everything that has happened, nothing surprises me anymore.

Famous quality Browning Company had me endorse their graphite fishing rods. But they wouldn't manufacture my fishing lures because they were too difficult to make.

They did make a bass lure and promoted it extensively. But it ended up a dud (didn't sell well).

They easily could have sold large numbers of my lures because everyone has always wanted them due to all my national publicity, and with their famous name brand.

Bass anglers participating in tournaments at The Gorge keep the bass they catch alive in their boat live wells until they weigh and release them at the marina. Then my children, Lisa and Kirk, liked to catch them and take them home and eat them.

It remains overwhelming to me, all of the things that have happened in my life... impossible for so many in one lifetime.

A most major one remains the death of my father in my arms while a young teenager.

We were working together laying bricks and blocks building the new Millcreek Stake Center in Salt Lake, when we jumped off a low scaffold to go eat lunch.

Unknown to us, rebars had been drilled into the cement floor that morning. My father didn't notice one and he jumped directly onto it. The safety caps had not yet been put on the rebar tops.

He fell on one, impaling him through his chest near his heart.

Seeing medical personnel first repeatedly shock him in vain trying to keep him alive... with blood all over me and holding his bloody wallet... my being right next to him as he fell, then holding him in my arms as he died... influenced all the rest of my life. I am certain much of my and my five sisters' lives and our mother's would have unfolded much differently if he had not died at that time like that.

I thought I was a "one girl kind of guy." But the first girl I wanted to marry was killed by a friend of ours from high school with a butcher knife while I was on a church mission, because she wouldn't go out on any dates with him.

My first wife died from cancer after we were married. When I proposed to my second wife, she cried and told me she would love to marry me but couldn't because she had cancer. I told her that didn't matter to me, and I married her anyway.

She was the kindest, sweetest person I had ever known and had a spiritual aura enveloping around her that instinctively attracted everyone that met her. She died less than three years after we were married from exceedingly painful bone cancer which literally ate and dissolved her bones away.

My third wife ended up dying from excruciatingly painful Lou Gehrig's disease.

My first daughter, first child, died during childbirth. The third child, a daughter, likewise died.

My fifth child, another daughter, also likewise died.

My grandmother died from a heart attack when I was a baby while holding me in her arms and dropping me as she fell on the big stairs of the old Wasatch Plunge swimming pool. I was at my mother's side when she died from intestinal cancer. My father's dad died while living with us in our house.

My sister Patricia died from lung cancer even though she never smoked. My father's brother Lester was killed in World War II. My father was wounded with seven bullet holes on Iwo Jima when all but a half dozen of his marine group were killed in the force that raised the famous iconic American flag there. He spent two years in a hospital recovering before being returned home.

Two people I was fishing with drowned and died in front of me when their boat turned over. I found myself in bitter cold winter water in the middle of the huge lake in very big waves with heavy snow falling... without any life jacket.

I had never swum the length of a swimming pool in my entire life.

I should have died by all scientific and medical explanations… but I didn't.

I was in cold water barely above freezing icing over for many hours. When finally rescued, medical personnel said I should have lost consciousness and died within a few minutes from hypothermia and drowning. They said I swallowed so much cold water that my body was bloated and my core temperature far below any possibility of survival.

The result was a feature article in *People Magazine* (at the time usually featuring movie stars and famous politicians like the Kennedys.)

Many stories continually circulate around about me. Some true… some not true. Many claim I also hold the world record for killing, drowning the most people in one day… because of the boating accident.

National magazines have loved to call me "The Hermit of Flaming Gorge" and "Modern Day Cave Man" as a result of my sleeping in a cave several months a year during the cold winters while fishing (only returning at week's end to go to church on Sunday). They also delight to take pictures of me bathing through the ice to keep clean during the week.

Jealousy amongst fishing guides, none of whom have ever been featured in a single national magazine, has always remained fierce.

One day, a national magazine crew had fished with me and caught and filmed some very large fish. They took them all over the small town of Manila, Utah showing them to everyone in the stores, service stations and cafes.

When they left, I drove my boat to my storage garage and backed it in. Two jealous guides shot multiple shot gun blasts into my storage unit through the walls and door, destroying my vehicle's roof, windows, seats, etc. I should have been killed… but wasn't.

The sheriff deputies never arrested nor charged them, because they were friends (as usual). The Manila Sheriff's Department said they have a very high thick file of dozens of incidents against me and my family, yet they have seldom prosecuted a single person who has done anything to us.

In this instance, they claimed I did the shooting myself to get more publicity. Absurd, ridiculous.

The bullet holes in the walls and garage door of my storage unit did become a tourist attraction for many years, with many people coming to see for themselves and take pictures.

A small prison was built close to our home on the end of our hill with the hope of earning the small community a lot of money.

One Sunday, when very few guards were on duty, two notorious well publicized convicted murderers held there walked out the front door and escaped.

For several days, hundreds of law enforcement personnel searched for them for some fifty miles around. Commercials were run constantly on TV offering a very large reward. Airplanes and helicopters constantly flew all over looking for them in the hills. Their scent dog only followed their trail the short distance to the road right in front of the prison, then lost it, so they thought, decided the escapees must have been picked up by a vehicle.

While the search parties were looking for them mostly 30 to 50 miles away, my son and I had our hunting camp, tent, sleeping bags, etc. just across the street on the first hill right in front of the prison.

That day while we were a couple miles away the inmates escaped when we were in church. They simply walked straight across the field in front of the prison along a fence line bordered by small trees. And walked up the first hill where our camp was, found it, stole everything and subsequently used our camp gear to stay warm and dry, eating and drinking our food... successfully avoiding capture for several more days.

The next day we went back up to hunt at our camp and found everything gone, missing. And found the escapees' footprints where they went.

We immediately went back down to the sheriff's department and told them and offered to take them up there ourselves to show them where the inmates went.

But they didn't believe us. They thought we were just lying to collect the reward.

Days later the escaped duo was finally caught while ordering a pizza at a pizza shop, after holding our hunting knife at an old man's throat at his cabin and stealing his truck. They found all of our camping gear belongings in their possession in the stolen truck they were driving.

They never paid us a penny of the large reward nor even ever gave us any of our camping gear back. Yet we were the only ones who knew and told them and offered to show the sheriff's department and marshals service where the inmate killers went when they escaped.

I have always filmed all the fish I have caught. Besides usually fishing in boats, I have also fished a lot off shore, especially during winter when the boat ramps are often covered in ice and snow.

I took the opportunity to get unique special film, video footage during a rare total eclipse of the moon.

I parked miles from any people or buildings and began to walk down a steep remote mountainside to my favorite place to cast off the lake shore. It was bitter cold but a full moon in the dark of night. I desperately wanted to get that special video footage of the eclipse of the moon, so I continued walking.

I fished through the night. The fishing was excellent, and I got great video and film footage and also still photos of all the different phases of the moon eclipse... holding each fish I caught up against the moon before letting it go.

Suddenly I had a very hard strike which pulled me forward forcefully, off the edge of the bank into the deep water.

My back was toward shore; my feet couldn't touch the bottom. I couldn't turn around nor let go of the fishing rod because the reel and handle got tangled in the big net I had hanging over one shoulder. And I had my large camera case over my other shoulder.

I was sinking deeper swallowing water in the bitter cold lake with the large fish pulling me farther from shore... but I couldn't do anything to help myself... except pray. Somehow I got back onto the shore and back up to my car.

I started shaking violently from the intense cold. I couldn't walk nor even stand up from severe cramps and uncontrollable shaking.

My gloves and snowmobile suit sleeves were frozen. I couldn't use my fingers nor hands.

I was so unbearably cold I couldn't stop shaking violently. Long hours passed and I still couldn't get my gloves off nor drive. I had filled my tank full with gas just before I drove down to the lake. By the time I was finally able to drive away, the gas tank was nearly empty.

When my wife Virginia died, after being unconscious for weeks, I was holding her in my arms sitting with her on her hospital bed. She hadn't been awake, talked, nothing for days. Suddenly her eyes opened, she kissed me, thanked me for marrying her in the temple... then died. I don't have adequate words to express how I thought and felt. Then it was a troubling contrast... people just outside the room door in the hall were laughing. When the orderlies came and zipped Virginia's body into a rubber bag and carried it away, it seemed shockingly disrespectful and blasphemous.

Each time my several children died, I felt I couldn't bear it.

For many years, I have walked two or more hours daily for health. I had just returned from a temple endowment session and was an hour into my walk when I felt wet on my forehead and face. Blood was running out of my head profusely.

I didn't know why. I thought I had been shot by antelope hunters who were nearby as I had just heard several shots fired. I still don't know for sure, but I had two deep grooves across my forehead.

I was able to walk back home where I was dumbfounded to see how much I was bleeding in the mirror. I stood in the bathtub, and it was filling up fast with squirting and dripping blood.

My son and wife drove me to the closest hospital where they immediately informed me I had a heart attack and must have fallen face down onto the rough road asphalt I was walking on... splitting my forehead open.

I didn't at the time and still today do not remember falling down nor getting up, if I did. It seems much more likely to me that the two horizontal long deep grooves in my forehead were made by gunshots from the antelope hunters close to me, not by the smooth level road surface. They said all seven heart arteries and veins were totally plugged and all needed replacement.

However, they only replaced five of the seven because they were afraid it would kill me to reach the other two behind my heart.

So, I am still at risk of strokes or another heart attack with those.

For many years, I slept in a small cave under a huge boulder on the lake shore during the bitter cold winter months, while fishing for the famous record brown trout. I put the boat cover over the cave entrance to help keep more of the cold wind out. It was too windy often to keep a tent from blowing down even if tied up to trees every which way with ropes.

This place is 2,000 to 3,000 feet straight down at the bottom of sheer giant steep cliffs.

Suddenly one night while I was sleeping in the cave, it felt and sounded like the end of the world, an enormous earthquake and thick unbreathable dust with rocks rolling on top and all over and around the entire area.

When it was over, I tried to crawl out for a look—but couldn't. The cave entrance was totally blocked, filled in and covered over with rocks... some gigantic boulders.

It took hours of extremely difficult work to move enough rocks to crawl out through a small hole. The entire area was a giant rockslide. And the 3,000-foot cliffs above showed large sections had fallen off.

My boat tied to the shore was filled with boulders and almost sunk. I was ten miles from the closest access point, road and marina. How I wasn't killed defies belief, logic.

This little cave is where I wrote my book *Big Trout*, which all printings have sold out.

Over the years national magazines have often filmed, videoed, and photographed many varied wildlife right at my cave, while documenting me living in it. Including wild Rocky Mountain Sheep walking through the cliffs dislodging rolling rocks right above my cave; mountain lions; moose; elk; deer; coyotes; otters; bald eagles; golden eagles (most just across the other less steep shoreline the other side of the lake).

A mountain lion killed a deer less than 20 feet from me while I was sleeping one night.

Of course, the main wildlife of interest to photograph always still remained the fish. More huge famous trophy brown trout have been caught by me in one short block long stretch of Flaming Gorge Reservoir directly in front of my cave than have been proven ever caught by anyone anywhere else in the world in history.

That is the reason I became nationally and world famous. It never could have happened with any other species of fish. The brown trout has been considered the "aristocrat" and holy grail of sport fish... the most difficult to outsmart and catch and the rarest in truly big trophy sizes.

Unfortunately, I could only catch very many of them during the coldest winter months, which required extremely difficult endurance and suffering.

The closest rival for that fame is the legendary "Musky"... which species world record I also hold (Tiger Musky)... also caught within my home state of Utah... in Pineview Reservoir. I, my children, and my wife have caught all of our world and state record fish on my fishing lure I invented.

I invented my fishing lure when very young, trying different samples nearly every day except Sundays in Big Cottonwood Creek just below our Murray, Utah house.

What would you do if your government kicked you out of the country of your birth and refused to let you ever return or enter again the rest of your life?

Man without a country. That was me.

My father was a decorated war hero Marine who fought in World War II on Iwo Jima. He promised me my entire life as I grew up that I would never have to go to war: "Because he did all of that for me, our family, and our country."

Also, having had two sons die, I was his only remaining male child who could have children to preserve his name and continue his posterity.

Read the scriptures, and you will see how all-important it always was to everyone to have at least one son to continue the family line and name.

But even though I was truly an all-American boy in every sense, the United States Government revoked my citizenship, left me outside America forever and refused to ever let me enter again.

My father fought and helped to preserve our freedoms against real World War II threats against our homeland.

I was drafted into the Vietnam War. What good did it do our country?

Since I didn't want to kill anyone who wasn't directly attacking our homeland nor my own family, and because I was the only surviving male to carry on our name and posterity... and since the Army labeled me unfit to be around any loud sounds... and since I entered the amnesty program and worked for free in that alternate service, you would think the bureaucrats would have been satisfied.

But no! They weren't.

I had gotten very good grades all through school. I was a clean-cut Christian churchgoing fellow who never smoked, drank, used any drugs, never committed any crimes... but I was "famous"... very famous, at a very early age, starting in my teens.

They wanted to make a well-publicized example of me against all those others who didn't want to support the Vietnam War. So I returned to Finland.

They issued me revocation loss of my United States citizenship... "a man without a country." "Miracle of Miracles," I received a totally unexpected phone call one day from someone I didn't know and of whom I had never heard. Chris Wanesgaard said he was an attorney with one of the largest law firms and they wanted to represent me against the government and the army... for free.

They had watched the news coverage about me and felt it was most cruel and unfair. He stated he had been a military prosecutor in Vietnam for years, but now he felt treatment of some U.S. soldiers was unjust... like me: For some dozen years, they represented me.

I had to take out Finnish citizenship to get back into the U.S. which resulted in my being drafted into Finland's army.

I got back into the country, eventually, though I was sent to prison.

They kept me from being deported multiple times. They succeeded in my not having to pay huge fines to the Army. But they always said there was little or no chance of ever getting my U.S. citizenship back. They also warned me never to go outside the country or I wouldn't ever be able to get back in again.

Many years later, my wife and I received a phone call, totally unexpectedly, from Chris Wanesgaard asking us to come to their attorney's office immediately.

He didn't say if it was about anything good or bad. My wife was afraid after all those years we had lost the court case and they would deport me.

But no, we, he, they had won the court case completely. My citizenship was reinstated (actually the court declared that the government never had the right to claim to revoke my citizenship in the first place... so I never lost it to begin with).

I didn't have to pay any court costs, no fines, nothing. The government was ordered to expunge my record and issue me a passport and allow me to go in and out of the country freely (from without a country back to famous patriot).

My father always told me that I would never have to experience the horrors of war as he did on Iwo Jima, because he and his brother suffered all that for the rest of us.

Also, my parents lost two sons to death, leaving me their only living son. So, it was illegal for me to be drafted, as the sole one who could continue our family name and posterity. But I was drafted anyway.

Also, at basic training the army doctors issued me a permanent profile not allowing me to be near any loud noises, which made me useless for war and military service. They said they drafted me anyway just to count me in the quota, because our church was getting so many exemptions for missionaries.

I also did not want to kill anyone nor war against anyone not directly attacking my family nor my homeland.

That did not go over well nor end well. The army court marshaled me and tried to imprison me for seven years. But the convening officer judge dismissed the officer jury, said that was totally unjust in my case, and lowered my sentence to just a misdemeanor and bad conduct discharge and only nine months confinement... no felony, no long multi-year prison.

However, I had already been held in the Ft. Dix stockade a long time before my trial, which was the first time I had personally seen homosexual sex.

Finally, I was handcuffed to a convicted murderer and transported one night across states to Ft. Leavenworth, Kansas.

Immediately three tall large black inmates told me I was going to be their new girlfriend. I would rather die than be raped, so I fought them off. The guards came and put me in solitary confinement for my own safety. Every time they later tried to put me in joint cells with other inmates, I successfully convinced them to always leave me in a cell by myself.

I could not believe any place in America so horrible could exist as Ft. Leavenworth prison. Many prisoners there had sex with girls in Vietnam then killed them. Many had fragged their sargeants and officers in their tents in Vietnam (thrown hand grenades to kill them). The blacks, Puerto Ricans, and Spanish speakers all had their own protective groups who watched out for and defended each other. The only whites who did were the lifers, all there for murder.

We shorter term whites were alone, undefended. I was certain I would be killed and never get out. The warden made me his clerk to do all the typing.

Finally, I was released... with an old suit on my back and a bus ticket only half-way home.

I had seen inmates killed right next to me with groups bashing their heads repeatedly against the tile communal shower walls, and throwing others to their death over the cell block tiers' handrails. I see protective screening in prisons on TV. There were none, only low handrails, at the longest existing American prison which was the civil war prison long ago, where I was.

When as a prisoner I was being transferred from Ft. Dix, New Jersey to Ft. Leavenworth, Kansas prison, handcuffed to a murderer, under military guard, when an uncle and aunt of mine walked up to greet me in the airport.

Surprised to see and hear my situation would be a vast understatement.

Lieutenant William Calley who ordered the My Lai Village massacre of all the women, children, and old men in Vietnam was incarcerated with me at the same time, in Ft. Leavenworth, Kansas. He was there only a short time before they transferred him to a private motel room to protect him from being killed by the prisoners where I remained.

I was always hungry the entire time I was in prison. I didn't drink coffee nor tea, so only drank water. The army had a big scandal at the time about their meat purchaser buying bad meat. I risked nearly every day stealing food in the chow line because I was so hungry. More time would have been added to my sentence if I had been caught.

I learned to play cards and chess well during rec time nights and bet my rations of cigarettes which I never smoked against the other prisoners' candy rations to get more to eat (and often won).

Lots of bugs like cockroaches infested my cell. Every third day for eighteen long hours we short termers were forced to do KP, kitchen duty, which was horrible.

Most prisoners ran out, smoked all their cigarettes, before they were issued their next rations. They craved their "smokes" more than candy so many lost their candy to me.

Many of Finland's military personnel rode bicycles in summer's warm weather and skied during the cold snowy winters when in service duty. They famously held off the much larger Russian army when Russia tried to invade Finland.

I was drafted into Finland's army after taking out Finnish nationalization citizenship to get back into the U.S. after the U.S. revoked my U.S. citizenship... which leaves me now, after my U.S. citizenship has now been restored, with dual citizenship of both countries.

Famous Pittsburgh Steelers football player Jack Lambert invited me to stay with him for a while in Pennsylvania at his very nice house. We went fishing together, out to eat, and held news events for the press... both of us Hall of Famers.

I showed films of many of the largest brown trout ever filmed being caught and released at sports shows and conventions all across the country yearly on one screen... and close-ups of my lure's fantastic wiggling on another screen.

Like at the largest salmon club's annual banquet in Chicago... where I was invited to be a guest of honor and feature speaker, advertised to be there on TV, radio and in newspaper and magazine ads.

That resulted in dozens of invitations to fish with lure companies, charter boat captains, famous people and other well-known fishermen in their boats all across the Great Lakes which was fun. Virtually all of them were astounded, stunned, at how well I and my lures caught fish.

Many different people and magazines have always tried to credit my angling successes to just my personal skills, not to my lure's effectiveness... claiming I could have caught just as many fish on some other lures because of my experience and knowledge.

Ridiculous! I know and have proven for decades that I could not have caught most of my fish on any other lures, baits nor jigs. With dozens of lines out in boats all over the Great Lakes on flat lines, planer boards, down-riggers, outriggers right next to mine at the same times in the same boats, my lures have always caught more fish than any other lures... and often all caught those days, with none being caught on any of the other lures next to mine, side by side.

Our family's entire life, day after day, at Flaming Gorge and many other lakes, we have been the only ones to catch any fish or very many, while sur-rounded by dozens of other boats, and have been the only ones to catch any trophy or world and state records those days.

My children and I have caught dozens, scores of Tiger Muskies at Pine-view casting our lure off the shoreline banks, with guides and pro anglers right in front of us in their boats casting their different lures right on top of ours... with us catching the only ones caught, daily.

Even in derby day contests at The Gorge, I and my children have averaged catching fish every five minutes or less, while we have seen very few if any caught by any of the dozens of other boats surrounding us.

Kokanee Salmon eat microscopic zooplankton, not minnows nor crawfish, but we have caught hundreds of them trying to eat or kill my lure... including dozens of world records.

We have caught more than a dozen varied species of birds catching my lure to eat it, and a mink, all on video... accidently, unexpectedly, both casting and trolling.

While trolling (pulling the lures behind the boat) at Strawberry Reservoir, my children have always liked to keep their lure close behind the boat and motor where they could see the fish swim up and grab their lure, competing who could catch some the closest.

I have done the same thing fishing for big muskies on Lake Erie which are often attracted to the motor prop wash turbulence, and on Lake St. Clair.

Muskies are notorious for following lures and baits right up to boats or the shore on casting retrieves without biting.

I, however, have almost never seen any muskies follow my lure without grabbing it in their mouth trying to eat it.

When little, I dressed like Huck Finn and often won the children's fishing contests on Huck Day, catching the first, the biggest, and the most fish.

Poison oak and ivy grew many places along our creek, so I often caught it.

I got tired of living in Salt Lake and working there then having to drive 200-plus miles back and forth each way to go fishing for the record trophy Flaming Gorge fish.

So, I talked my wife Joyce into moving up there. She applied for a school teaching position in Manila High School in that small community and was accepted.

We picked out a house to buy and live in.

Right then the two guides shot my boat garage to smithereens nearly killing me.

In addition, some jealous fishermen out on the lake several times pointed guns at us threatening to shoot me.

Also, our two young sons, Clint and Kent, had just been sleeping with me in my boat garage barely before the shooting.

Although Joyce was used to living in a small town having been born and lived in Gooding, Idaho... because of the shootings she became too scared to live there.

Years later when I married Jolene I finally got to live there near my fishing. I bought an old mobile home and fixed it and its yard and the dirt road up the hill to it... and we lived in it thirty years, raising Kirk and Lisa there.

They were able to and did participate in all of the many school activities in Manila including learning to use computers well.

They also had jobs to earn extra money for themselves, like Forest Service projects, town office grounds maintenance, painting, weed spraying, lawn mowing, building ponds and fences... a whole lot of different things.

Lisa learned to drive big trucks and tractors. I also bought them both the most expensive ATVs which they enjoyed riding all over before they were old enough to drive on the highways. They could not have done that in a city.

At our home in Manila at The Gorge, I built a very large bird house on an old unused telephone pole and big hoot barn owls lived in it for years.

Lots of geese fed in the field next door.

Next to our yard lived a large colony of prairie dogs. Chipmunks, squirrels, lizards and lots of cottontail rabbits also lived in our yard. We saw both red foxes and coyotes daily and often bald eagles, golden eagles, and falcons. And of course, lots of deer everywhere. Many would jump our high fence around our garden. Some were so tame they would drink water right out of the hose in my hand. We often saw Rocky Mountain big horn sheep and elk walk by.

In their schools when asked to write about who their "hero" was, my children always said "their dad"... not because of being famous, but because I dared to keep getting back up on the high scaffolds working despite my father dying in my arms and all of the many other accidents I and co-workers next to me suffered on the scaffolds.

One good result of raising my children in the very small town of Manila, Utah way out in the country far from any other towns or cities was always much more opportunities for them to participate in school... in sports, plays, music, dance, computers, etc.

My father, while in WWII on the island of Iwo Jima, where his Marines raised the famous flag, received word of his second daughter Patricia's birth with this announcement: "Marine on Iwo Jima learns of his new baby girl while hunkered down in a fox hole on battle rocked Iwo Jima. That is how Marine Corp. Delbert L. Johnson, 22, received the glad news (amongst all the deaths)."

He was the radio man with guards in front and behind him, to protect him and help roll out the phone wires to other troops.

He said he knew the spirit of the Lord and guardian angels were with him the entire thirty-two days he was on that death island... amid the constant machine gun fire, explosions, and flame throwers all around him.

Nearly everyone close to him was killed. He had to crawl through blown apart body parts, gore, and blood to unroll the phone wires over countless dead bodies, for weeks, day and night, 32 days.

Iwo Jima had the highest casualty rate of all the World War II battles. All but a small handful of his group were killed.

He prayed constantly keeping prayers on his lips, non-stop, he was so scared.

In Finland the weather was so cold when Russia invaded Finland, that film shows hundreds of Russian soldiers instantly freezing standing up when hit by bullets, their dead bodies still standing upright not falling down, as their warm blood left their bodies.

Most of his life, I, his son, was the only person my father would tell anything about his dreadful war experiences. Mom occasionally heard bits and pieces from his nightmares while he was sleeping.

Even though he was still quite young when he died, he was in so much pain from his seven bullet war wounds that some people thought his accidental death was a blessing to relieve his pains. We never heard him complain though.

My dad and I were genuinely best friends and enjoyed doing everything together, work and play.

He was the only person I ever saw who bartered in every store for lower prices in return for paying cash. It embarrassed me, but it often worked.

He was a busy guy. Besides his constant church service long hours, he often stayed up late at night going over construction masonry plans, figuring out how much to bid, charge on building jobs.

He loved to fish and always took our whole family nearly every Saturday.

He enjoyed hunting big buck deer. Robert Redford was not the real Jerimiah Johnson.

Since I was only five years old, my father, my uncles Hyrum and Mike, and I took the three- to four-hour hike up to the very top of Timpanogos Mountain near Emerald Lake, hunting the unusually big bucks there... in bitter October cold and snow.

We had to bring the harvested deer down the backside literally over the cliffs to the Timpaniki Trail... very difficult. I have spent much of my life for many years atop Timpanogos Mountain... not Robert Redford.

Before real downriggers became known or popular, I invented and used my "minnie downrigger"... a heavy weight on the bottom of my rod's line with my lure on a dropper line above it. I would occasionally let it down to just barely touch bottom briefly then lift it up a few feet to keep my lure trolling close to just above the bottom without snagging.

Occasionally I would snag up and lose, run out of the weights. So, with a national magazine I invented tying a rock in my white handkerchief as a substitute weight, with one end corner of the handkerchief loosely waving in the water.

That attracted fish so well that from then always after we tied even the lead sinker weights inside a white handkerchief to attract the fish.

My children have enjoyed catching and eating crayfish by hand wading, with traps, and on their fishing pole lines with a piece of chicken. No crawdad ever saw nor ate a chicken, but they love it. We just eat the tail meat, not the whole crayfish critter.

All in one day by my cave, George Lelis and I caught eleven trout each over 20 lbs. mostly browns but also one huge rainbow and cutthroat... which would not have been any unusual big deal if they were just lake trout; but an unheard-of miracle for browns, rainbows, and cutthroats at Flaming Gorge or anywhere else in the world.

Most anglers have never caught even just one anywhere near that big their entire life.

George Lelis's friend, Paul Mazuran, who owned a sporting goods store in Murray, Utah, used to fly us in his plane up to the Gorge to fish together in his boat which he kept at the little Dutch John airport.

He frequently let me fly his plane. He had a nice cabin we slept in on the Ashley, with dozens of different souvenir decanter liquor bottles decorating the walls.

One trip he invited me on I couldn't fly up with him because of scheduling. So, I told him I would drive up and meet him there. But he never arrived. Unfortunately, his plane had crashed. I was supposed to be on it.

Another friend was supposed to meet me at the lake but never showed up. He slid off the winter ice off the road down into the steep Carter Creek Canyon above Sheep Creek.

A different friend also didn't show up at Lucerne one day. He had hit a deer driving fast and totaled his expensive sports car.

Probably the most famous fishing lure inventor was Lauri Rapala from Finland (where I went on a mission).

By coincidence, I was inducted into the fishing hall of fame together with him the same year... but I for record fishing success more than for inventing my lures.

However, I think I have more than adequately proven that my lure invention catches fish better and more often than any other lures.

The only reason mine haven't been sold so widely world-wide is because they are so difficult to manufacture.

We are exploring the possibility that the new photo printing machines may well make that much easier.

For many years we caught those big lakers when they were spawning almost every pass over the spawning hill in October and December.

Then lots of anglers started illegally snagging them anchoring their ropes all over the hill preventing us from fishing there at all anymore.

After years of our complaints, fishery officials finally closed some spawning beds for both lakers and kokanees to protect them from the illegal snaggers, especially during dark nighttime hours.

Our family's many constant complaints finally succeeded in getting both Wyoming and Utah fisheries to close those species' spawning areas to lessen the illegal snagging.

I have never liked other anglers illegally snagging kokanees, lake trout, nor salmon anywhere, as many do on both Flaming Gorge and all around the Great Lakes.

We have seen many trucks and boats on trailers slide backwards into the lake water during winter on the icy snow-covered ramps while trying to launch their boats.

People have reported, claimed I had drowned several times. Another frequent false tall tale is that I have supposedly been banned from ever fishing the lake again for using live goldfish illegally (not true, of course).

One Spring water flooded the Sheep Creek campground and drowned several people camping there.

A short distance away by Flaming Gorge Lodge a forest fire killed several fire fighters. A memorial has been built there in their honor.

Not far away is a monument and fenced grave tourist attraction where an old cowboy is buried with his horse. He asked to be buried sitting in his saddle on his horse... and he was.

The famous Flaming Gorge fishery now faces likely extinction due to deadly algae bloom ballooning in warm weather poisoning much of the water's oxygen content... so bad on parts of the upper shallower lake portions that it often forms a solid layer on the surface that fishing lines can't be pulled through.

Also, invasive mussel species multiplying also threaten the water quality and fishery. Illegally planted burbot have increased beyond control also taking over the lake, drastically reducing the cray fish, minnow, and zoo plankton foods for game fish.

The lake became famous for its original trophy sized brown trout, but they almost totally disappeared long ago, due to too few being planted and their food supply being destroyed.

Either illegally planted lake trout or ones that migrated down the Green River from upper Wyoming lakes totally took the lake over long ago, drastically depleting the chub populations on which the game fish fed. They used to exist in the lake in vast schools but very sparse populations now remain.

Much of the upper lake portions are surrounded by oil shale and such a high oil content some places that the rocks can literally be set on fire simply with a match.

The Green River below the dam is famous for its fishing but nearly all its trout are now very small, not trophy sized like in the past.

Coors Beer Company ran its famous long running "You Can Call Me Ray" ad campaign as a parody of me, since I don't drink alcohol and wouldn't endorse drinking their beer (for which I could have received lots of money).

My wife Joyce slept with me over Easter under a picnic table catching big browns, rainbows, and lake trout herself that trip.

We used to paint the lures we used in a "frog color pattern"... but the paint would eventually rub off from the fishes' mouths, so we found out that most fish bit just as well on the unpainted original pale-yellow color out of the mold.

It is interesting how I, we, have changed our color preference over time, from "frog" to silver to white to yellow. It doesn't seem to matter to most fish, as we have caught lots on red, orange, purple, black, and gold colors as well.

I have long been credited with originating, inventing, discovering and catching trophy sized brown trout trolling in the dark of night, when they are not as difficult to outsmart as during daylight hours.

I have always caught the vast majority of them when dark enough to need a flashlight to net them and floodlights to film them... most during the early morning hours just before daylight while their chub forage fish are feeding on the surface.

We have also caught a great many big lake trout in the dark of night as deep as 120 feet trolling my littlest two-inch size lure three miles an hour fast.

It is doubtful they can even see it down there in the dark. But my lure's frantic wiggles create water disruption vibrations which the fish can feel with their lateral line to locate and grab it in their mouth to eat it. However, they find it they bite like crazy in the dark.

Because even a few samples for our own use have always been difficult to make, I have seldom had very many myself.

On one occasion, Joyce and I snagged the last lures we had with us on the bottom and accidently broke our lines and lost them. Remarkably I was able to snag them and get them back with a stronger hooked line. Incredibly we then quickly caught a couple of record fish on those lost recovered two lures minutes later.

Famous long term KSL TV sportscaster and bridge tournament champ Paul James caught so many and such large fish with me that he ran full features on their TV newscast every day for a week, and also mounted several on his home wall.

Famous BYU coach Stan Watts was presented a mounted fish he caught with me I had taxidermized for him, at half-time of a game at BYU.

One of the many rumors, stories widely circulated about me actually believed by some people is that I drowned in a boating accident. Another is that I died and my ghost skeleton is still seen standing up trolling in my boat back and forth the one block stretch by my cave.

The Red Canyon Lodge at Green Lake has a small pond they let little children catch rainbow trout in, most very small. But they also put one great big trophy sized rainbow in there that none of the kids seemed able to catch.

But my little son, Kirk, caught it, his very first cast on my lure with his little kid's pole. He and his little sister Lisa caught lots of others also out of that children's pond.

Because of frequent strong winds the only way to prevent damage to our motors and boats is to tie them with three ropes against the shore, one to each side as far away as possible from each back corner, plus dropping an anchor down also in back of the stern.

When my wife Virginia died from bone cancer, one TV station had a very nice lengthy tribute about her and her life.

My children have loved walking the lake's shores beach combing for lures. Lake trout anglers snag lots of them trying to fish close to the lake's bottom. Then when the hooks on the lures eventually rust, many float to the surface and are washed ashore by the wind and waves. We have found and collected many hundreds of them over the years. Of course, we have often spotted many other things also, like wallets, hats, lifejackets, and all kinds of garbage.

There is a rich history around the lake including Butch Cassidy and the Sundance Kid's hideout and other outlaws, and early pioneers' cabins, and lots of dinosaurs. Rare trumpeter swans are often seen on the lake.

Big crowds have often greeted me daily at the boat ramps when I've come in from fishing to see or hear what I caught and take videos and photos and selfies with me and collect autographs.

Unlike all the bass tournament anglers, I don't wear product company endorsement patches all over my clothes.

People who don't have good fishing success often accuse me of having already caught them all...but I release them all.

Despite the lake's famous trophy reputation, the big fish are only caught in a few small areas, not throughout most of the lake. I have often said, "I think a person can fish longer without catching anything at Flaming Gorge than any other fishery I know about."

I have been surprised for years how many people keep showing me photos they believe show UFOs they've seen, and aliens.

Many readers of my book *Big Trout* have told me they have never laughed so hard. To know my true complete life's history, you need to read my fishing book because it includes many hours of details about much of my life.

I have often bought a couple of my lures back from other anglers when I have lost mine and ran out.

Some critics have called me "stubborn"... but I like to think of it as perseverance, grim determination. Writers say I "will the fish to bite my lures."

It seems like most people have always either hated me or loved me... not neutral.

Few things in life are ever as good in reality as people hope. But many things in my life have been far better than I could have ever expected or wished for. I have been able to do most things I dreamed of and wished.

I recently reread my book *Big Trout* and was surprised how many details and descriptions I included when I wrote it, with a pencil on paper in my cave while fishing.

My mother put fish, carp, buried in her flower gardens for fertilizer which I caught down in the creek just below our house.

I built a small concrete pond in our backyard lawn in which I kept fish, frogs, toads, snakes, lily pads, and watercress.

Behind our neighbor's house in their field, one of their sons, Govert Copier, and I built a small barn and dozens of pens we raised all sorts of animals in: Guinea pigs, hamsters, rabbits, pigeons, pheasants, quail, chickens, white mice and rats, gerbils, and magpies (we taught to talk).

We had so many Guinea pigs in our barn that they ate two big bales of hay every day. Plus, we got old left-over produce, carrots, lettuce, and all other kinds from grocery stores (for free) to feed all our animals.

We had every different color combination of Guinea pigs, chickens and pigeons, including little banties and big fighting cocks. We had both roller and tumbler pigeons, pygmy rabbits and giant rabbits.

My parents got us children a couple of little yellow ducks, which grew into enormous giant white creatures as big as geese. They terrorized the neighborhood and chased all the dogs and cats (and people away).

At our former home in Springville, Utah, I used to catch fish, trout, right out of the tiny irrigation ditch in our yard. I also accidentally set our shed on fire there.

We had lots of reunions with all our many relatives... in church buildings during cold winter months and outside up canyons during summer... always with dances.

As a young boy I fished in Big Cottonwood Creek almost every day, where I invented and developed my fishing lures.

But I also caught suckers and carp which several oriental neighbors enjoyed eating, especially the sweet tasting suckers' meat. They paid me a lot for them since they were not sold in stores.

When our dad first built our home in Murray, Utah, there weren't any other homes nor businesses anywhere nearby.

There were deer in the fields many months of the year, and coyotes and porcupines.

Now it is the center of a big city with buildings close together for miles.

For a long time, I kept a big tall teepee, which I made myself, on our back lawn that I used on some scout outings and our children often slept there.

Eventually homeless camps along our creek, especially near the Jordan River, made our young kid treks very scary and unsafe... with all the drug needles to step on and outdoor bathroom waste.

I played the flute in school, in orchestra, and also in the youth symphony. Also played it in church meetings.

I never had any piano lessons, but most of my sisters did. I taught myself to play the piano and eventually played all the music for most of my life in church meetings and on my multiple missions.

I've never gotten as proficient on the piano as I've always desired however. I can't seem to move my fingers as fast as my eyes, or something. I am amazed at how beautifully fast my wives Virginia and Joyce and my daughter Lisa played.

I bought Joyce an expensive piano and loved to listen to her play.

My parents loved to dance, both ballroom and square dances. In those days, the church held monthly dances for both adults and youth separately in our stake.

My oldest sister Barbara and I were the dance instructors. I also decorated the gyms for dances, dinners, and holiday parties. I also performed floor shows.

Our parents sent me and my five sisters to dance classes, both tap and ballet.

I danced on several TV shows, starting with *Uncle Rosco's Children's Show*. I was also selected to be "the lead" in multiple performances and reviews. My mother hoped I would earn my living by dancing.

My father filmed everything with an old 8mm. There are hours of us dancing on his films.

I followed by filming all the state and world record fish being caught by myself, my wife, and my children. I've always used newer film and video equipment, however.

Except in the early days out in the sub-freezing cold at my cave catching the world-famous trophy brown trout, some photos in my book *Big Trout* were taken with a little instamatic camera.

I lived all those winters sleeping while fishing without any heat, in often below zero cold.

I also drove my boat repeatedly through ice to get to open water fishing spots, when the ice wasn't too thick to break through.

Besides writing and selling books, I have also made and published fishing maps of lakes. My beautiful Flaming Gorge Map has sold tens of thousands of copies. All of my book printings have sold out. Because I was a national and world-famous angler, I was invited to fish both with famous Finnish and Swedish and Russian individuals and government officials, sometimes in private or restricted famous waters, the various times I lived in Finland.

Finns used gill nets besides fishing rods and lines to catch salmon, northern pike, burbot and unusually large yellow perch. Fish were a large part of many Finns' diets.

The outdoor markets offered many fish for sale.

When young I dug tunnels long distances in the vacant fields around our house. We children loved to crawl and play in them. While digging I found both dinosaur bones and Indian burial remains next to our house which we took to the natural history museum.

A next-door neighbor boy, Ronald Esmeyer, and I flew his gas-powered remote-control airplanes a lot and had air war dog fights with them trying to knock each other's plane out of the sky with our own plane.

We also made rockets and shot them into the air... until we got in trouble from one coming down through the roof of a house.

We built go-carts with lawnmower engines and drove them all over the roads and subdivisions. There wasn't hardly any traffic by our house for many years. We played in the middle of the roads all the time.

We eventually graduated to tote goats (mountain motorcycles).

We also built many makeshift boats and then floated in them down Big Cottonwood Creek from below our house clear to and far down the Jordan River many miles away.

Later we got and used canoes.

Back then there were lots of fish in the big creek... mostly brown trout but also lots of planted rainbow trout. Of course, lots of carp, suckers, chubs, and minnows also. But many perch, bluegills, walleyes, big and small mouth bass, white bass, and goldfish also ended up in there... some illegally planted by neighbors and others migrated up the creek out of the Jordan River and Utah Lake.

Two boys floating down the big creek during high spring runoff flows fell off their inner tubes in front of me in rapids. I swam out, rescued them, and literally saved their lives from drowning.

While swimming (reaching hands in under the stick snags to hand catch fish) I found dead bodies with bullet holes in them, on multiple occasions (very creepy).

I enjoyed playing most of the different sports. Back then the church held tournaments for lots of them: basketball; volleyball; ping pong, etc. I was pretty good at all of them.

In school the coaches wanted me to run track races because I had run the mile in four minutes in practice. I also was the fastest in cross country.

Eventually it was suggested that I try out for the Olympics... but then I was drafted into the Vietnam War... then I was imprisoned.

Instead of completing military service I entered the Amnesty Program. I worked at the original Salt Lake Cannery.

Besides canning food, they had me repair all the buildings' masonry.

After I had already worked in the program (for free) the government notified my attorneys that they finally decided that I didn't qualify for the program.

I always hoped to make my living selling my lure invention widely. But that became difficult due to lack of start-up money. Also, the critical intricate balance of the lure to achieve all its fantastic wiggles was difficult to manufacture.

So, I ended up most of my life laying bricks and blocks, building houses, churches, businesses, and university buildings, just as my father did all of his life.

When young, he was a chef in a California restaurant and always wanted a restaurant of his own... but never got it. He contracted masonry construction instead.

Today young people aren't allowed to work in America on dangerous construction jobs.

But my father took me on the job sites working from a very early five-year-old age. First, he had me do the striking... which is finishing the mortar joints between the bricks and blocks to look nice, tooling them.

But soon by age eight he started teaching me to lay, place, the bricks and blocks in the mortar... paying me. At age ten, I worked every summer, all summer, plus Saturdays all year with him on his job sites.

By age twelve he was paying me $10.00 an hour. And soon after I was paid the same as his long time adult workers.

I hated the cold conditions of winter outdoor working, with the old "Salamander" oil heaters.

But that is what I've ended up doing all my life... working in the bitter cold of winters and scorching heat of summers... with the intense sunshine reflecting off the walls.

I have helped build so many different buildings I can't remember them all. Here are some of them. Shortly before I retired, just a couple of us built the new natural history dinosaur museum in Vernal, Utah. One of the last was the new Murray High School buildings in Utah.

But I've built all across the country; also, I've worked on churches all across the Hawaiian Islands. Also, Lowes, Sportsmen's Warehouses, Home Depots, and others in several states.

Others are: Piccadilly's Fish; McDonalds; 7-Elevens; tire stores; print shops; banks; various other businesses; many churches; several fine arts centers and many other university structures on numerous campuses; many different hospitals; and lots of schools; plus, hundreds of individual houses; also, apartments.

Building sites are often dangerous, as my father's death on a rebar in my arms and many other personal accidents during my life attest.

In Yuma, Arizona, one summer's heat simmered so unbearable that they had personnel squirt us workers with hoses all day long, constructing a new high school.

While laying the top block courses high up on the new gym, the forklift operator accidently dropped a heavy load onto the lofty scaffold which collapsed it, falling from under our feet.

I jumped on top of the fresh wall we had just laid which was still very weak, while most of the other workers next to me fell to the ground and were rushed to hospitals.

While constructing the Olympic athletes' condominium apartment housing for the Salt Lake Olympics on The University of Utah campus, an exceedingly rare tornado for the area hit us directly.

A roofer above me slid over my head off the roof to the ground and his death. Part of our scaffolding collapsed; the rest swayed violently with many of us, including me, way up high far above the ground.

While building a Moran Eye Center Hospital, also on the U of U campus, a welder on the roof accidently dropped a very large heavy wrench which hit the top of my work helmet a direct blow, far below him where I was working, destroying my safety hat. Luckily, unexplainably, I wasn't killed.

A very strong thin line is used stretched as tightly as possible to lay bricks and blocks along, to keep each course level without any sag belly curve. Wood blocks are used to secure each end of the tight line secured on square corners (leads) and metal pins stuck in joints otherwise.

Occasionally someone accidently brushes or bumps a block or pin, releasing one end of the line suddenly like a shot arrow. I have been hit by the fast-flying blocks and pins many times, severely hurt by them. I have suffered teeth knocked out, my nose broken, bad cuts on my face, arms, fingers, and body.

I was often the only one who passed every frequent drug test on the job sites.

I always had a job because I always did perfect beautiful masonry work. I often did the most difficult parts and most difficult designs.

I was asked several times to build the brick display panels at the companies which manufacture and sell bricks. I invented many of the designs on houses and some building owners like on the two Maran Eye Centers on the U of U campus, I'm told that my employer got those big contracts because of the beautiful and fancy designs I did on their buildings.

We filled many block walls with dusty insulation we poured into the block holes. We also breathed constant dust from the brick and block saws making cuts.

Nearly everyone except me smoked all day every day right next to me. The doctors at my openheart surgery told me all of that smoke and dust probably caused my heart attack and plugged blood vessels.

Even though my mason's pay checks were fairly high, I never got any health insurance nor other benefits.

I worked for Lee Ingersol when I got out of prison. Then for many years I worked for Mike Knudson at Heritage West Masonry. After that, for many years I worked for David O. Anderson Masonry.

In recent years lucrative contract bids have been difficult to win locally in Utah, due to so many new immigrants bidding lower. So, I had to go all over the U.S. to do buildings in several states… away from home months at a time.

Some of the jobs in Hawaii I did for Ron Almond.

Masonry is not only physically difficult, constantly lifting heavy things all day, but is mentally fatiguing. It requires constant math, measuring and leveling and plumbing... keeping everything perfectly straight and perpendicular.

Laying out the first bottom courses, measuring all the door and window openings and setting them precisely, placing exactly all the electrical and plumbing pipes and fixtures and metal roofing support plates inside the masonry walls... all requires constant exact math calculations as well as making intricate exact fitting brick and block cuts around all the fixtures.

I also worked a lot with several close relatives; Hyrum, Joe and Ronald, three of my father's brothers, in both Utah and California. Also with several other relatives, in California.

Uncle Joe was the church's plantation foreman supervisor for more than a dozen years in Hawaii. Just before my father's death, he was interviewed by the church to move to Hawaii for five years to be the buildings' supervisor. Our family was preparing to pack our bags.

Afterwards I built our church buildings and additions and repairs all across the Hawaiian Islands.

Many of my co-worker masons over the years were very big, tall islanders, much stronger than me. Blocks are very heavy. It was difficult for me to raise them up high above my head over the rebars to lay them.

But I was usually faster than many of the others. Lots of them drank coffee and energy drinks constantly and took pain pills (and who knows what else).

Chemicals in the mortar lime and cement can eat your skin and flesh away over long exposure, so most masons always wear gloves. Due to the rough abrasive brick and blocks holes quickly rub through. I often used two pairs of expensive gloves up daily.

My uncle Ronald didn't like wearing gloves… and he really suffered for not doing so. Eventually his fingers were drastically painfully damaged, for the rest of his life.

High mason scaffolds are made so that a two-foot gap remains between the foot planks workers walk on and the material planks behind them, to enable the walkway to be raised and lowered.

It is easy not to notice where you step and to accidently put your foot and leg down the hole while moving back and forth working fast. I have seen co-workers even break their leg doing so.

Nowadays, stricter safety rules and protective gates and personal safety harnesses are usually employed… but not during most of my career. I have witnessed numerous workers walk off the end of the scaffold walk blanks and fall to the ground, resulting in their death or serious injury.

One otherwise tragic such accident became a truly hilarious comedy when a worker next to me walked off the end fast not looking while singing and doing the "moon walk." The rest of us just could not stop laughing, since he fell unhurt down to the ground.

Brick bundles are held together with metal bands. One of our workers was turning pulling one stand of brick around (which is difficult alone) while building the new Sugarhouse, Utah library… when the metal strap broke.

He fell over the edge of the scaffold down to the ground, landing on sharp rubble which literally tore his nose off, broke several bones and lacerated his body severely in many places.

An unlucky guy, later he was hit by a train while crossing the tracks with an equipment truck and trailer, suffering many broken bones and very serious injuries.

I saw one worker cut three of his fingers off while cutting brick on a diamond bladed table saw. Injuries on those saws are unfortunately frequent. Much more dangerous are the hand-held saws, similar to chain saws, used to cut rebars as well as blocks. I saw many workers injured in their legs and bodies accidently touching themselves with the whirling blade.

One forklift driver went too close to an edge turning the machine over on its side. Somehow while it was rolling over, he was hanging partially out and it crushed and killed him.

In Modesto, California there were so many homeless guys all around us bothering us as we built the new soup rescue mission that our tools were stolen constantly if we didn't keep them in our hands.

Daily immigration officers lined them up checking for illegals. Shots were often fired close to us most days. People used the ground for their toilet all around us, and it was difficult to step anywhere without stepping on either it or countless drug needles.

A tall crane blew over in the wind ruining dozens of cars in the parking lot while we were building the new gym at Salt Lake Valley Community Redwood Road College, barely missing us.

The summer heat well over 100 degrees many days while we built the huge Lowes Warehouse in Redding, California resulted in virtually all of our masons who were sent there quitting and returning to Utah to other job sites... because they all fainted, couldn't handle the heat.

That left me alone with just one local young helper to finish the big building and the long retaining wall all around the property, in the scorching heat.

When finally finished weeks later, I drove straight through without stopping to sleep or eat back to my home in Manila, Utah.

While playing with my children, my youngest son Kirk noticed my left leg was swollen twice its normal size, and said I needed to go to the emergency at a hospital. The closest one was nearly one hundred miles away.

By the time we arrived there, the pain in my leg was excruciatingly unbearable.

The doctors informed me I had seven blood clots in my left leg and that I was very lucky I wasn't dead.

They gave me lovenox blood thinner injections for weeks, then cummadon. That was 16 years ago.

Ever since then I have had to take warfarin blood thinners every day. Also, as a result, I had a heart attack requiring open heart surgery.

I was driving back to work in Salt Lake after enjoying being home over the weekend and attending church with my family in Manila at Flaming Gorge when it snowed as I drove.

Just before Evanston, Wyoming are three big hills called "the three sisters." Between the hills on the lower highway stretches the semitrucks were still going 80 mph. But they had to suddenly slow way down to get up the steep long hills covered with deep snow.

I put my four-wheel drive Nissan Exterra in four-wheel and slowed way down to only 35 mph.

As I approached the top of the second high hill, four semis roared past me fast right where the three lanes turned into just two lanes.

The semi on my right suddenly swerved right in front of me, hitting the front corner of my vehicle with its back corner, flipping me around... right into a car.

Then another car hit me while my SUV was sideways pushing me into the guardrail. When my vehicle quit sliding, I was pinned by the airbag which exploded out of the steering wheel. And the dash had been caved pushed back against my chest and legs.

My face and chest were bleeding profusely. A nurse from another car helped get me out. She also saved the lives of two elderly people in the car my vehicle was pushed into when I was hit from behind by yet another truck... just barely seconds before that couple's car was hit on the side pancake smashing it like a flattened stepped on tin can.

Then and ever since, and still, I have always been so grateful that they were not killed by my SUV being pushed into the side of their car from behind... even though it wasn't my fault, nothing I had control over.

Lots more cars and trucks kept driving and sliding into those of ours already wrecked as they crested the hilltop.

Deep snow covered the road on that hill, and heavy snow kept falling. It was difficult for me to walk even a few steps. But the nurse helped me walk the short distance to look over the hill crest.

What an unbelievable sight. As far as I could see, both sides of the multi-lane highway were completely covered by stopped, sideways wrecked cars, trucks, and semis.

On my side, the four trucks had topped the hill and plowed into already stopped sideways vehicles.

I was extremely cold; my vehicle was totaled, and I couldn't run its engine nor heater. No ambulances nor police cars could get through all the wrecked vehicles on either side of the highway for more than four hours.

No helicopters came either in the blizzard falling snow. I was frozen stiff. When an ambulance finally did reach us atop the hill, the paramedics put me, the elderly couple, and as many others as they could fit inside and started treating us.

I later heard from news reports that the massive pile up accident was one of the worst in Wyoming's history... for number of wrecked vehicles and deaths.

My Nissan Exterra was totaled. The exploded safety bag took lots of skin off my face and my ribs were bruised badly. My chest and legs had been crushed by the dash forcefully pushed way back against me. I never missed a single day of work and was never late a single time all my life. Since I lived hundreds of miles away most of those years, I slept for more than 50 years in my work cars and SUVs, in the backseat... mostly in parking lots; returning home only for weekends... saving lots of money over renting motel rooms.

Before she died my mother let me stay with her for a while since my father died. My sister Janet let me sleep nights at her and her husband David's home for a while.

Most of the time when my job sites were close enough I slept in the parking lot of a printing copy shop, where both the owner and manager gave me permission to sleep for many years.

Some other places I used were often rousted by police or attempted robbers (which happened frequently). I defended myself against robbers hitting them with my hard four-foot level several times.

My dad's youngest brother, Ronald, liked to hobo ride trains around the country. He kept asking me to go with him. So, on a lark, I decided to try it just to see what it was like.

We ended up several states away and it took us days to get back to Utah. I disliked all the hobo camps we stayed in.

When young, my children loved to be out in the windy waves on our boat... the rougher, the more they liked it. They always fell asleep despite the lurching boat movements in the waves.

Most fish feed and bite best when windy waves stir all their food up and lessen the sun's light penetration in the water.

So, I have always been the last boat still out on lakes fishing after everybody else goes in as it gets too windy for them.

Some varied other experiences from my life follow. While living in Finland after my mission there when I returned, I worked for a while at the ship building yard in the warehouse giving out all the different materials to the workers building the big ships... from little screws to big sheets of metal.

This was interesting because it required quite good use of the Finnish language. I had never learned nor studied any language before going to Finland on a mission. And at that time there was no language school for that language for missionaries.

I was just given a small dictionary and a few photo copies of basics to learn. I read street signs everywhere I went, read the scriptures in the new language (which I was already familiar with because I had already previously served an English-speaking mission).

The Finnish words are exceedingly long with add-ons both in front and behind many words. It seemed impossible to learn at first. But after only a few months I was able to say virtually everything I wanted to and understand most spoken to me.

A different job I did for a longer time in Finland was as an assembler of metal shelving on job sites all over Finland and Sweden. It required welding on some jobs, from metal stairs to securing rails to floors for carts to run on holding shelves.

Some nights I was locked in bank vaults with all the money while installing new metal shelves.

One night while installing extensive carts on tracks shelving in a morgue with all the dead bodies, suddenly a body next to me moved a lot. I found it difficult to concentrate the rest of that job. It felt creepy.

I even cleaned offices for a while at a different job, at night when they were closed. I wasn't used to the smell of coffee grinds, and I didn't like the smell, as I cleaned coffee pots and mugs.

I also taught English-speaking lessons in Finland.

In Salt Lake City, Utah I worked once for Mr. Mac, of TV commercial fame, selling suits and missionary clothing. He finally fired me, because many fisherman fathers and sons came in his headquarter mall downtown store "asking for me to wait on them"... aware I was the famous angler they had heard so much about, wanting to meet me, get my autograph and take a selfie with me.

Mr. Mac hated that. He was used to getting all the fawning attention himself in his own store, from all his TV appearances and as tabernacle choir director.

My oldest sister Barbara and I were the clerks operating "State Stone" when our father and family opened it in Salt Lake. There we sold different colors of marble and various other rocks from our mine in Nevada. At the mine I also got to set off dynamite explosion blasts.

State Stone is still open operating, but we don't own it anymore. We sold it after my father's death.

Our family has paddled both canoes and inflatable rafts on many hikes into mountain lakes... even in Yellowstone Park, like at Shoshoni Lake... with both grizzly and black bears often close to us within sight... and also down the swift rapids of both big and little rivers, like the Snake.

While in Hawaii one of my many times there, the Hawaiian King and Queen often invited me to eat with their family... and to go wading in the ocean surf and tide pools catching shellfish, finned fish, eels, and crabs with our hands.

They and their children would eat most of the creatures they caught right then, on the spot... raw! I never managed to convince myself to do that.

They wanted to manufacture my fishing lure invention there in Hawaii. But I didn't want to move or live there permanently, as my father's brother Joe had done, managing the church plantation there.

Joyce and I had a three-month honeymoon in Hawaii, after a few days at Disneyland, Marineland, Knox Berry Farm and other California attractions.

She broke her wrist completely through both bones falling slipping on coral while we were searching for shells at the Kona Beach.

No hospital was close so we went to and had it cast by a veterinarian at a large farm. They gave her laughing gas, and I had never seen nor heard anyone laugh that much and loud. I even caught a huge sea turtle on my lure. Most ocean fish species have readily tried to eat my lures.

I have been the guest of honor at many dinners, conventions, and high-level meetings where alcoholic toasts have been raised... but have never hoisted, drank, nor sipped mine. I have always asked for a glass of water instead, and have never been embarrassed for doing so.

I have always voted my entire life.

On one of our explorer scout camp trips a champion high school swimmer with us tried to swim out to a floating log raft drifting in the middle of the lake to retrieve it to shore... got cramps and drowned.

With no phone (wouldn't have been reception anyway) and no horse, we had to make a stretcher to carry and drag his body the entire eight miles back down to the trailhead from Granddaddy Lake in the Uinta Wilderness Area.

As a scout I only achieved "Life" rank, not Eagle, despite lots of merit badges, because I thought I was too busy to take the several week swimming classes required at that time. That was a mistake. My youngest son, Kirk, did earn his Eagle rank.

I have been a merit badge counselor for several badges and also been an assistant scout master.

On first dates with my wives, I have surprised them with a whole room full of roses and other flowers and cards and posters. Once unbeknown to me, a TV station was alerted and showed up to film it all.

Except with one, who was a blind date referred by one of my sisters. She answered her door to see me wearing a big diaper dressed as baby Howie on Halloween.

Lisa, my only daughter (the fourth girl and seventh child of mine) who lived, was born May 29, 1991. (She served a mission to Santa Rosa, California.)

My first son, Clint Ray Johnson, was born October 31, 1980 on Halloween (my first child was a girl who died before his birth).

My second son (my fourth child) was born August 3, 1983, Kent Ray Johnson.

My third son (and sixth child) Kirk Ray Johnson was born December 20, 1989 (served a mission to Minnesota… where our great, great grandfather Aaron Johnson went on the first mission there with Joseph Smith, mentioned in the D&C, and first mayor of Springville, UT).

My wife Virginia's parents, Essie and Willis Candland, provided us with a new duplex to live in with furniture and lots of other things when we were married (they already knew their daughter had terminal cancer).

Virginia decorated all the food for every meal in fancy shapes, really neat, even vegetables with nuts and fruit. Her father was both a general contractor and one of Utah's largest sheep producers, in Mt. Pleasant, Utah.

He with his neighbor captured the then world record black bear on the Manti Mountain Foothills behind his house, practically in his backyard.

I was accidently shot with a razor-bladed arrow while deer hunting, bleeding so badly we all thought I would bleed to death. Nearly a hundred miles from the closest hospital we phoned asking if there were any paramedics closer. We were told only a husband-and-wife couple. But when they finally came, they informed me they didn't dare treat me because they were "drunk." By the time I finally got to a hospital, the doctors said it was amazing I didn't bleed to death.

I have always bought brand new four-wheel drive SUVs for all of my children while they have been living with me.

When I traveled to sport shows yearly, from coast to coast (from San Francisco to New York), I always exchanged the money I made to a paper bank draft before I left each show... and put it inside my stocking inside my shoe on my foot... to lessen losing it to robbery, which attempts unfortunately were attempted.

I was seriously stabbed with a knife once and had guns pointed at me a dozen times, both robbery attempts and jealous fishermen out fishing in boats.

Porta-boat company took me all over the country to promote their boats, also.

Though I am their competitor, I was paid $10,000.00 by the Rapala Company which makes and sells Lauri's lures, because of publicity in national magazine articles about me in which I plugged their lures.

My sisters are: Barbara, born Jan. 24, 1942 in San Francisco, California; Patricia, born Feb. 1, 1945 in Payson, Utah; Janet born March 19, 1951; Karen, born Nov. 7, 1956; and Jeana, born May 21, 1961 (all in Salt Lake, Utah).

My mother's great grandfather, Ray Averett, caught live wild animals for zoos. I was named after him. He captured bears, cougars, etc.

My father, Delbert Leon Johnson, was born: Aug. 23, 1922 in Salt Lake City, Utah. He died Nov. 21, 1964 in Salt Lake City (from an accidental rebar through his chest when I was sixteen years old).

Lavern Gourley Johnson, my mother, was born Jan. 28, 1924 in Springville, Utah. She died April 25, 1992 in Salt Lake City from intestinal cancer.

Mom had 2,000 flowers in her gardens around our house…the most beautiful yard anywhere. Roses were her most favorite.

Outside, she loved flowers and grew extensive rose gardens and all types of other flowers, with various varieties of grape vines all over along our backyard fence.

She and all our neighbors paid me for many years to catch all the gophers with traps in their flower gardens to prevent them from eating the roots and killing their plants.

Wherever our family went to Yellowstone Park, in the mountains, to zoos, out to our Nevada mine…our mother knew and told us all the names of all the plants everywhere.

She crafted every imaginable handicraft, from doilies to dolls to quilts to everything else…which she both gave to everyone as gifts and also sold. She even made her own potato chips.

Dad constantly put his arm around her and told us children: "You have the most beautiful mother in the world."

She was beautiful, gracious, kind, and loving to everyone.

Both of them sang all the time and were happy.

She took us every year out to our Nevada mine to pick lots of pine nuts to roast, eat and sell.

She made éclairs, puffs, cakes, all types of cookies and fancy candies, as well as the best most tender roast and better than most hamburger pizza. She also loved both halibut, shrimp and chicken. She also frequently fried corn dogs, fries, onion rings, and deep-friend desserts.

She helped me make the decorations for many dances, dinners, and birthdays and wedding receptions…and cute costumes for me in all my plays and road shows.

She always called me "ray of sunshine" … since her other two twin boys died.

She had six children who grew to adulthood, five girls and me, one boy (her only son still living). She also had twin boys with blonde hair and blue eyes like me, who died.

All three of my daughters who died had strong heartbeats right up to the moment they popped out…but evidently didn't survive the birth stress. No doctor was ever present, only trainees. Each time they told us afterwards the babies could have lived by taking them cesarean.

It devastated Joyce so much she refused to let go of their bodies and give them up. She also had a miscarriage. She was already older before she had her, our, first child.

My daughters' names who died are: Ann, Jenna, and Joy…buried together in our family cemetery.

When my wife Virginia died from bone cancer, one TV station had a very nice lengthy tribute about her and her life.

I married Jolene Okelberry December 28, 1988 in the Salt Lake Temple. She is still living.

I have often wondered how it is even possible that all this started and happened in my life.

My father was in the Millcreek 8th ward bishopric for 19 years… as clerk, counselors and bishop.

He was always extremely friendly and loving to everyone, putting his arm around them greeting every person with a hug and handshake.

He was a fun-loving guy who sang everywhere as he went, even when working… often crooning very old songs like: "She'll be coming around the mountain." He also joked all the time.

Everyone just loved him right back. When he died, an enormous standing room left only crowd attended his funeral.

After having so many die, it has always been indescribable joy each time one of my babies and grandchildren have lived.

We discovered before unknown petrified dinosaur tracks in the newly exposed shoreline not far from my cave when the lake water level lowered to an unusual low.

We also found lots of big dinosaur footprints in a very difficult remote access area near our hunting camp.

I helped start the world record "release alive" program at the Fishing Hall of Fame, as well as Utah's state release record program.

My children and I used to hold the state Utah released fish records for almost every species of fish in the state.

Because I am so famous, some skeptics have asked me if I would ever be willing to give up all that fame and attention.

It is a very significant thing to be called "The One Very Best in the Entire World in all History" for decades, by dozens of national magazines and The Hall of Fame… as they have acclaimed me.

In school I drew and painted huge murals on the long hallway walls, of Indians riding horses shooting running buffalo with bows and arrows… in beautiful colors.

The night before my father died, he took each of us children aside alone in our own bedrooms... and blessed us and prayed with us, instructing us for our future... as though he had a premonition, he would die the next day.

I have received an abundance of love from my children and grandchildren, running and jumping on my lap and hugging me tightly. I have also felt the deep precious love of a loving wife... every touch and heartbeat.